CW00660889

the Courage to Ask

to Ask

Cultivating Opportunity in the New Economy

John Niland & Kate Daly

First published in 2012 by
VCO Global
7 Pound Close
Blunham
Bedfordshire
MK44 3NR
www.vco-global.com

A CIP catalogue record for this book is available from the British Library

ISBN 978-0-9572493-0-1

Lovingly created by Infinite Authors

Printed in Great Britain by TJ International Ltd, Padstow, Cornwall

MIX
Paper from
responsible sources
FSC
www.fsc.org   FSC® C013056

Contents

Preface

This book was born in scary times. Our five characters are fictional, but all the events described are very, very real.

We know... because many of them happened to us.

When we were introduced to each other, via one of our clients, we had little idea of the turmoil that the following year held in store. A series of tornados hit each of us: successive waves of business upheaval and family crisis that may well be the subjects of another book one day . . . when we acquire sufficient time and distance to write it.

Along the way, we learned some important lessons about courage and about asking. In our conversations with clients and friends, we also found we were not alone. Many professionals were going through their own storms. We are particularly grateful to them: for the inspiring conversations along the way, for the courage they demonstrate as leaders navigating the choppy waters of today's marketplace.

That's enough about us. This book is about you, your friends and family. It's about the better conversations we all need to have for prosperity in a new economy.

John and Kate

Foreword

The marketplace we service has dramatically changed over the past five years and our consultants and managers have had to adapt to this new climate.

Whilst we initially engaged Kate Daly and John Niland for different reasons, the synergies between the two have been tremendously beneficial. Using her organisational expertise, Kate supported Bluefin Solutions to define development programmes and identify the precise talents necessary for future success and growth. In parallel, John coached and trained key individuals on advanced consulting skills. Even our most senior consultants found the VCO approach eye-opening.

Across both domains, the issues of 'courage' and 'confidence' kept arising. It takes courage and confidence to give (and receive) feedback. Most consultants can document requirements but it takes a courageous and confident consultant to challenge a client's thinking. It takes courage and confidence to formulate a future business or project plan when many variables are unknown. It also takes courage and confidence to adapt a plan when necessary, and equally, to stick to one with persistence in the face of obstacles and setbacks.

So it made sense to introduce Kate and John to one another. At Bluefin Solutions collaboration is key to our approach, so we really understand the strength and value of it. I am delighted that their collaboration has been tremendously valuable.

By continuing to invest in and encourage the development of individuals, Bluefin Solutions is in a stronger position to adapt to ongoing challenges and changes in the SAP marketplace and to ensure that our customers continue to get the best possible advice and service from us. There is no doubt that 'courage' has been integral to this.

Philippa Holland,
Global Consulting Director, Bluefin Solutions

Part one

Part one

1
The Case for Courage

'I couldn't wait for success… so I went ahead without it'
– Jonathan Winters

The ultimate purpose of this book is to support you, the reader, to create opportunity: both for yourself and for other people. Without opportunity, your talent could be one of the world's best-kept secrets.

Across the world, both young and old are in need of opportunity like never before. Traditional escape routes such as emigration, further education or reliance on others do not serve today's professionals as they served previous generations. Today's marketplace calls for greater courage.

For quite a few decades, society has focused more on developing *expertise* than developing *opportunity*. The assumption was 'develop your expertise, and you will always find someone who needs those skills'. But 'the times, they are a-changing'. Many highly qualified professionals are now more in need of *opportunity* than of expertise. But, being so accustomed to developing expertise, they may not see this clearly.

We are writing this book now for three reasons. First, we all live in a new reality, where the return of good times won't bounce us back into a previous life where skill acquisition dictated success. Second, many people need levels of courage for which they have not been prepared. Third, today's reality demands that we create opportunity from fewer resources. Simply talking about abundance or skill does not create opportunity, we have to do something more.

We are going to explore in some detail the single 'foundation skill' of *asking*. Why? Because the ability to make requests defines those initiative-takers who make opportunities *happen*. If you don't ask, the answer is always No.

Opportunities are 'openings' to add value, and hence to create prosperity for ourselves and for others. Without the capacity to ask questions and make requests, most strategies to add value and create opportunity are just dreams, even if written in business language. They're never going to happen.

Many people know this, it's just common sense. So... how many 'asks' are you doing, on average, each day? How many requests did you make today, since this morning?

Asking takes courage. Courage is the capacity to act in spite of known fears, risks or uncertainty, whether actual or imagined. The key phrase here – often overlooked – is 'the capacity to act'. Courage, very broadly, involves making a decision or taking action. Businesses and organisations often seek to add value, and hence create opportunity for themselves, by focusing on skill development. Yet 'the capacity to act' involves more than skill.

The development of skills (and competency models in particular) has dominated literature, research and practice for over thirty years. Skills can be taught, knowledge can be gathered and behaviours can be learned, which is why these models are attractive and have persisted. But while skills can be taught, unless these skills are *utilised* – that is, 'acted upon' – nothing changes. Courses are forgotten, training manuals gather dust and organisations remain the same. Courage is the catalyst for change – that is to say, courage is required in order to put skills to use, and ultimately to create opportunity.

'If you don't risk anything, you risk even more' (Erica Jong). Courage is the necessary force for ensuring growth rather than retreat. So before we roll up our sleeves and dive into the detail of this book, we would like to begin by *making the case for courage in business*.

The word courage comes from the French root *cour* or *coeur*, which means 'heart'. So courage has to do with the heart, the pump – that vital muscle that keeps our blood flowing and sustains life. Without the pump nothing thrives. Courage is called upon when the pump is needed, when our 'resources' are challenged or pushed to the absolute limit.

Most of this book is about courage. And asking, of course. Through a variety of characters and 'gateways', we are going to explore how different people with different personality characteristics can access the courage that is essential to cultivate opportunity and lead others to develop and grow.

Why courage?

Given that we could have written this book about many other aspects of leadership or business development, why did we choose to write an entire book about courage?

Adding our experience together, we have spent five decades in talent development. We have lost count of the sessions we have run with leadership teams, sales teams and professional firms, not to mention the thousands of hours of individual coaching that often follows these proceedings. We have seen hundreds of people leave events with new skills and confidence, ready and willing to develop, to create opportunity and make changes to their behaviour.

So... what usually happens? When we meet again, what do they report? Obviously, there are many who report progress and achievement; otherwise we would be out of a job long before we got to write this book. But equally there are many professionals who provide highly sophisticated explanations about why they could *not* do what they so confidently committed to doing, often only a week before.

In the course of our experience, we have become convinced that the dimension of *courage* is more crucial than the dimension of *skill*. Without courage...

1. People cannot achieve:

- Professionals cannot even use the skills they *already have:* for example, giving difficult feedback to a client or colleague. Like the farmer who said to the adviser, 'Please don't tell me how to farm any better; I'm not even farming as well as I know how already.'

- Vital decisions get postponed, procrastination takes over. To cover up, they call for more information and consultation, often making unnecessary work for others to disguise their own fear of making vital decisions.

2. They cannot open doors:

- They cannot initiate those meetings that are vital for getting jobs, presenting new propositions, opening doors or reaching decision-makers. They will *prepare* for the meeting, but will baulk at making the call to ask for it.

- They cannot follow-up the new contacts they have made, or the people with whom they have connected on social media. So they will complain about 'not being connected to the right people' when in fact they are not making use of the connections they already have.

- They cannot stay in touch, not even with the people they already know, far less those that they would like to meet. As a result, their reputation diminishes as time goes by; they simply get forgotten.

3. They cannot manage themselves:

- They cannot deal with setbacks and disappointments, which are the daily diet of anyone whose career involves opportunity creation. As the salesman said to the trainee, 'If you are afraid of risk, stay in the car.'

- They have difficulty dealing with uncertainty and lack of control; yet opportunity is rarely controlled by any one person. For people who need control, opportunity creation can therefore be a scary space, and scary spaces require courage.

- They cannot learn, because learning requires making the mistakes of a student, and many don't have the courage to do that. In the same vein, self-awareness also takes courage to develop, and as we will see later, courage also involves a degree of self-awareness.

4. Their focus is distracted:

- They are likely to put more energy into Plan B than wholeheartedly tackling the challenge of Plan A.

· They react to whatever comes up (emails, requests, tasks), because they don't have the courage to push-back and make space for themselves and their priorities.

· They suffer from 'hurry sickness', constantly rushing from one thing to the next, often because this is preferable to confronting the reality of their situation, which takes courage and honesty.

We could extend this list for many pages. The point we are making is that skill development alone – *without a corresponding shift in courage* – is unlikely to overcome many of the issues in leadership, opportunity creation or business development.

Even when conscious of this distinction, many will go ahead with skill development anyway. Perhaps they will pursue an MBA in the belief that this will give them more courage/confidence as a result. What usually happens? The more they learn, the wider the gap becomes. They frequently become skilled at strategising rather than doing, because this takes less courage. So the result of their studies is often less courage... and sadly, often more debt.

In our work with individuals and teams, we have found that by emphasising courage development as much as skill development, there are several positive ripple effects.

First, professionals *continue their learning* after the event, and usually improve on the tools and techniques they have been given. We find this particularly in the arena of business development, where courageous professionals take particular delight in sharpening dialogue skills and improving these skills long after the course is over, often becoming better at it than their mentors.

Second, they become eager to pass on their learning to others. By teaching what they are learning, a learning culture develops in a low cost and pragmatic way. Not only does the return-on-investment come from those who have been directly 'taught', there is a ripple benefit when they start to pass on skills to others. They become 'en-courage-d' in the very process of passing on their learning.

Third, they become more excited and engaged while doing so. Surprisingly, many personality types are more motivated by what they can *contribute* than by what they can *get*. Few organisations know how to tap this peculiarity of human nature. Many professionals are engaged by being challenged. They discover their strength when more is *asked* of them, rather than when more is *given* to them. They appreciate environments where limits are pushed and they feel they are growing.

Fourth, when courage grows, performance grows with it. Time management gets better, meetings get to the point, problems get dealt with rather than avoided. Results get achieved. Many performance-gaps are courage-gaps rather than skill-gaps, and we will see this phenomenon repeatedly illustrated in this book.

Winston Churchill famously remarked that 'courage is rightly esteemed the first of human qualities... because it is the quality which guarantees all others'.

Layout and structure

We've kept the conceptual stuff to a minimum; all too often, theorising cultivates *avoidance* more than it cultivates *courage*. Nevertheless, there is some essential 'substance' needed. Here is the structure we will follow.

The bulk of the book is about how to access courage, and we will outline seven 'gateways' that can provide this access. We will explore these gateways via five central characters; all in very different situations in their life and career. We expect you will get to know these characters rather well in the course of the book.

Though each of these five people is in very different circumstances, we will see it's their increasing self-awareness that makes various gateways to courage accessible. The situation in which they find themselves certainly plays its part, but even tough situations can be tempered by better awareness, creating new opportunity. When it comes to the 'courage to ask', it matters little whether one is an experienced consultant or a young jobseeker. The questions may be different, but the issues of courage are remarkably similar.

Along the way, there are various 'mechanics': the skills of asking, for example, which along with the gateways will hopefully be useful to you. There are also some exercises which we hope you will *do* (as opposed to just *read*) because courage, like fitness, cannot be built by simply reading about it.

Terms we use

We don't want to greet you with an academic-style lexicon. That's about as exciting as arriving at a party only to discover that you have to go through a five-page administration procedure in order to get in. But there are some words that we use a lot, and we are less likely to misunderstand each other if we take a moment to clarify the key ones now:

Courage: we define courage as strength in the face of risk, pain or grief. In the words of Ambrose Redmoon, '**Courage is not the absence of fear**, but rather the judgement that something else is more important than fear.' Courage may or may not be accompanied by confidence, which is a belief that we can make the best out of any situation.

Asking: primarily used in this book in the sense of making *requests*, that is, asking for meetings, asking for help, asking someone for information. However, there is an equally important use of asking (in English) which is the skill of posing questions – for example, 'Why is this important?' This type of asking also takes courage, and is an equally important skill for creating opportunity.

Gateway: When used in this book, the term 'gateway' refers to the seven gateways to courage explained in Chapters 9 to 16. All gateways are available to everyone, but some are more accessible for certain personalities than others. For example the gateway of 'Self-discipline' is usually accessible to conscientious people; while the gateway of 'Curiosity and Variety' is often more accessible to those motivated by openness and/or intellectual inquisitiveness.

Personality characteristics: When we use this term, we are referring to the Big Five framework of personality traits from Costa & McCrae[1] which has emerged as a robust model for understanding personality across all major cultures. As we will demonstrate, different personality types can access courage in different ways, via different gateways.

---

1. Costa, P.T., Jr. & McCrae, R.R. (1992). *Revised NEO Personality Inventory (NEO-PI-R) and NEO Five-Factor Inventory (NEO-FFI) manual.* Odessa, FL: Psychological Assessment Resources.

Change of behaviour

As many leaders will confirm, it's easy to change strategy, but a lot harder to change behaviour. We see the truth of this every day, and do not consider behaviour change as an overnight affair. Equally, there are key moments (often difficult ones) when courage makes a quantum leap. Perhaps a professional has been forced into taking an initiative that they dread, but in the act of doing so they find new reserves of courage that they didn't even know they possessed.

Or they find themselves out of work, job seeking in a difficult environment. In this context, 'opportunity creation' may be an unwelcome phase in their lives that they simply want to get through as quickly as possible, so they can go back to 'normal'. We hope this book will be particularly useful to jobseekers, because alas there is usually no training manager creating a budget for their development.

The need for opportunity is often forced on a person by circumstances, and behaviour change becomes a necessity rather than a desired outcome. These are the moments when self-awareness can grow, and when people can become conscious of their own strength. If this awareness can be reinforced and built upon, a difficult season can sow the seeds of a perennial harvest.

Let's meet some of the people for whom all of this is very real.

2

PlayStation (Adam)

'To live with fear and not be afraid is the final test of maturity' – Edward Weeks

Adam feels his mobile vibrate and glances at the number. It's Joe, for the third time today. He stares at the phone until it stops buzzing, then waits for the bip that indicates he has a message.

Another message from Joe, about a ski holiday that Adam cannot afford.

He sighs, drops the phone on the bed and stares out his bedroom window. On a Monday morning in January, how is it possible that a 28-year-old graduate of computer science is still sitting in his parents' house in Milton Keynes? Right now, Adam is too hungover to be angry. He crosses the room and fills another glass of water from the tap.

That was one helluva party. Emily will be annoyed. Oh well, he'll deal with that later.

As the water cools his throat, he looks down at the garden and glimpses the blurred outline of his father moving around inside the greenhouse. What does Dad think about? His father has gone very quiet since taking early retirement last year. At least he had a job from which to retire.

Adam sighs and checks the time on his mobile. Nearly noon. Soon time to face downstairs for another silent lunch with his parents and breakfast for himself. Silent with reproach for what he's not doing: finding a job. Coming home later and later. Staying in bed all morning. Not like Joe and Emily.

His parents don't get it. They don't understand that the 1980s were different. Back then, if you graduated with computer science, you might even be headhunted before you got your final degree. People of that generation talked about buying houses a year or two after they started work. But now, even for people like Joe who've been working for a couple of years, his friends are still years away from affording a deposit for even a poky flat in Bletchley.

No, Mum, it's not just a case of persevering. There are over one million unemployed young people in the UK alone. We are the generation that has been brought up to believe we can 'have it all', and now that we've studied and strived – often harder than you did, by the way – where is it?

Adam tries to estimate how many job applications he has made since graduation. God, that was four years ago! With hindsight, he wonders if he should have taken that year off, going around the world with Joe. They certainly had some experiences they won't be telling their mums about. Like that time in Peru when…

'Adaaaam, lunch time!'

'OK, Mum, coming down.'

OK, so how many job applications has he made since graduation? Counting the three years since coming back, Adam estimates an average of five per week. So allowing that on some weeks (like this one) he did no applications at all, he assumes forty active weeks per year… that's over 600 job applications in three years. That's probably more than both his parents did over their combined working lifetimes.

No, Adam has not been idle. He has taught himself C# and Javascript in an attempt to sharpen his skills. He has scoured classified ads both online and offline. He has written to countless HR departments of likely local firms as well as many further afield. He has attended graduate fairs and exhibitions, catching the train (off-peak) to London whenever possible. It's easy for those who say 'go to events', but do they realise that train fares cost money?

And the problem is always the same: no experience.

He has filled in more online applications than most people have booked airline tickets. And each application takes a lot longer than booking a ticket. He has even tried cold-calling some of the people listed on the job-boards. That was a waste of time; in most cases he just got voicemail. He has chased up some of the people listed as contact points in the adverts: just some of the many that never replied to his applications. He has mass-mailed unsolicited resumés to large companies that he was told would always be hiring computer science graduates. Well, they weren't hiring that week.

He used to get angry when people said 'Keep trying, don't give up!' On more than one occasion he and Emily argued about perseverance.

Ah, Emily. Adam sighs again, and puts down the glass of water. In his heart of hearts, he knows the game is up with Em. While they were both job hunting, they could share the ups and downs together. But then last September, Emily moved to London. She's now doing systems integration with an international consulting firm. One week she's in Leeds, another she's in Paris, all in top-notch hotels. Emily is ambitious; she works hard and plays hard. Adam doesn't dare to think about what happens in those expensive hotels.

It's amazing she hasn't dumped him already. Adam knows it's coming, and wonders if yesterday evening could be the breaking point. She became more and more furious as he got drunk with Joe on a Sunday afternoon, right in the middle of her weekend back home, too. Oh dear. There's trouble ahead.

'Adaaaam, you up yet?'

'Coming, Mum.'

Generation Y

Like many born after 1980, Adam is still living at home. Perhaps he doesn't feel the same urge to leave home as his parents did; home life is certainly more libertarian than it was twenty or thirty years ago. On the surface, no generation has ever had it so good... or so his parents think, anyway.

But dig just a little deeper, and we soon find a degree of angst that his parents probably won't understand. Assuming even a modest level of ambition, what's it like to be nearly thirty and still searching for your place in the world?

All over Europe, this is the lot of today's young professionals. Or, would-be professionals. Young people typically struggle to gain employment and are the first to be laid off; in nine countries more than one in four are currently without a job. Spain has the highest rate of youth unemployment, at 42 per cent, more than twice the unemployment rate of the next older age-band. In Sweden and

Luxembourg, the youth-to-adult unemployment ratio is more than four. Germany has the lowest ratio (1.3), often attributed to its unique apprenticeship system.

For young men like Adam, the effects are serious. Even if they have a supportive family, lack of opportunity not only impacts their economic well-being; it also affects their self-esteem, their confidence and their ability to relate to others in society. When Adam applies for the next job, what is he expecting to happen? In terms of his relationship with Emily, how does he see their future?

Adam is starting to believe he has exhausted all his options, and this is a very dangerous crossroads for a young man to be approaching. The last time this happened to a whole generation of young men in Europe was in Germany during the 1930s and the entire world paid a high price for their disillusionment in the years that followed, right up to the end of the Second World War.

This book is about discovering opportunity, and hopefully it will soon be obvious that Adam has not yet exhausted all his options. Nevertheless, there are three risks that we must name:

1. That no matter what, Adam will soon give up reading about opportunity, of any kind. His mother or Joe might buy him this book, but would he read it?
2. That even if he reads a book like this, he will lack the courage to implement it. Usually saying something like, 'that's fine for Emily and Joe, but it doesn't work for me'.
3. That his initial attempts to make use of the contents will be met with discouragement, further deepening his sense of failure.

If any approach is going to be of use to Adam, or any other jobseeker in need of courage, we're going to have to spend time understanding his world. It's far too soon to start talking about any so-called 'secrets of success', or telling war stories from our own experience. In this book, there are no secrets. Yet we hope there is some understanding, and a few gateways through which courage (and hence opportunity) can be accessed.

So – just in case you are impatient and curious – what do you think that Adam is **not** doing? Why is he not doing this?

Adam's world

Adam has been exercising consumer choice since the age of five. His entire upbringing has coincided with PlayStations, mobile phones, the Internet, text-messaging, Google, iTunes and Facebook. For Adam, virtual reality is not some 'other world'; it's what you use to access the rest of reality. When you want something, your intuitive response is to go online and find it.

You don't wait for the next publication or catalogue to arrive in the post; you Google what you are looking for. If you are searching for tickets in short supply, you don't go around tediously asking your friends, you just pop a question on Facebook. You don't wait for the weather forecast to appear after the news, you check it now on the BBC website.

In short, when you want something, you go online and get it. Right now. From a bus, a party, whatever. During class, in the middle of the night, whenever.

Adam has never used a paper diary or to-do list. Using his smartphone, his right thumb can find what's on TV tonight faster than his parents can locate the *TV Times* in their living room. His attention habits have equally evolved: he can watch TV, have a text-dialogue with Emily and check the weather forecast for the weekend, all at the same time. He laughs at his parents' stress about multitasking. For Adam, it's normal to be in several conversations at once.

Unlike his father, he has not lost contact with any of his mates from university; he gets their daily updates on Facebook. Of course, this means he keeps reading about their triumphs, successes, exotic visits and latest acquisitions. That's what Facebook is for, right? For some people, this might look like a super-connected world. For Adam, however, this is starting to look more like a world where he is being super-marginalised. And reminded of it, daily, too.

Adam's own updates have a light-hearted touch: underground comic videos, music, photos of bizarre people doing bizarre things. He steers clear of political causes, meaningful quotations and philosophy; that's just 'not his thing' – too intense for his taste. His status-updates give no clues about his underlying frustration. If they refer to his job search at all, it's usually an occasional humorous comment about some of the strange people who work in HR and recruitment.

If Adam is looking for a last-minute ticket to the O2, his 400-plus friends on Facebook serve him well. So why isn't this working for his job search?

Many people would suggest that he hasn't asked. Adam would reply that he has: he has joined LinkedIn and done company searches. On several occasions he has put out Facebook updates, indicating that a bright young graduate in computer science was still looking for a job. He has sent individual messages to people he's connected with, together with a nicely formatted CV attached. He has responded to job postings on LinkedIn. He has used Facebook to mention interviews he's had, or interesting people he has met. He has downloaded several guides about how to use social media for job search. And (doing his best to ignore the fact that many online guides seem to be just copies of each other) he has spent a couple of hours every afternoon (well, some afternoons) trying to follow their advice.

Finding a job does not seem to be the same as finding a last-minute ticket for the O2. Everything that Adam is reading: one million young unemployed, the growing influence of China, forecasts of lengthy depression, falling living standards, off-shoring of systems development… all seem to point to lack of opportunity, not lack of tenacity on his part. The advice he is getting seems to be applicable to some other world, not to his.

First steps

With all of this in mind, we might do well to tread carefully with Adam. His scepticism may not be evident behind his easy-going manner, but it's very real and surely understandable. He will naturally be wary of books like this one. Already, they seem to belong to another age: how to succeed in becoming another annoying know-it-all whom you wouldn't want to be around in the first place.

Yet this book is relevant for Adam. It's going to outline a simple way of finding – even creating – opportunity where none seems to exist. This will require new levels of tenacity and most of all, courage.

It's not that Adam's job search is defective. It's just that his upbringing and culture have not prepared him for what he now has to do: a lot of individual, one-to-one, conversations where he will be *making requests* and asking questions. And not just on Facebook and LinkedIn, though he will find those tools pretty useful along the way. There will be lots of *asking*, and lots of courage needed to ask.

To begin with, it will all be a bit weird. And about as attractive as going for a run on a Monday morning when you've got a hangover and you know you will be out of breath in fifteen minutes and wheezing like Grandad. You certainly wouldn't want the girl next door to see you in that condition. Nor Emily, come to think of it.

The parallels between running and 'asking' are significant. But rather than analysing these any further, or even reading any more, why not experience this first hand? Right now, Adam, even before you have your lunch. A short run, as slowly as you want, just for ten minutes. Emily won't see you; she's at work in Leeds.

Later on, we will see how many other changes too often happen from the legs upwards, rather than from the head downwards.

So don't think about it. Just put on any old pair of trainers, and go. That experience is worth more than a thousand words.

3

Sophisticated Procrastination

'I never put off till tomorrow what I can possibly do
– the day after' – Oscar Wilde

Adam is not alone. Nor is the need for opportunity confined to the young: there are many experienced people of all ages in search of new careers. We will meet some of them in the next few chapters.

Many of these professionals grew up in a world where the need for opportunity was no big deal. OK, at three or four (sometimes anxious) points in life, perhaps opportunity creation was uppermost in their minds, but most of the rest of their working lives was just about getting the job done, getting through their workload and getting on with their colleagues. Even freelancers and independent professionals could often disappear into interesting client assignments, and leave opportunity creation for another day.

There were easier things to do, more interesting challenges to ponder. Given two choices: opening up a new market (plus all the 'heavy lifting' this requires) or redesigning the organisation one more time, no marks for guessing what most managers/leaders chose to do.

As long as opportunities were plentiful, it was easy to put off opportunity creation until tomorrow. We could all carry on in our comfort zones. Even if a professional was bored with his career, or a manager could see a declining market ahead, there was usually something else that seemed 'more important just now' than creating new openings and opportunities.

Now all of this is changing, though many don't see the change... yet. Nevertheless, the career consequences are real, for nearly everyone in the marketplace. Why?

A globalised economy has certainly produced export markets for some industries, but has opened the floodgates to fierce competition for others. Ask a software developer anywhere in Western Europe where most of his day-to-day collaborators are based. Add to this a public sector that's tightening its belt, large private companies enforcing rigorous procurement and an economic outlook that's far from rosy. Companies need new markets, public organisations need new sources of funding and professionals need new clients.

On top of that, *supply of skill exceeds demand.* Everybody can have expertise at the click of a button or by watching a YouTube video. Moreover, many organisations want to do things for themselves. Gone are the days of blindly buying-in expertise – it's all about engagement now: working together to co-create results. Your skills are only the half of it. With few exceptions, most skill domains are oversubscribed, or soon will be as a host of professionals from emerging markets take the stage. Sure, there are still pockets of expertise in short supply: for example in the development of mobile apps. If Adam were to ask a bit more, to change his style of research and presentation just a little, he might well find them. But in all probability, even these skill gaps are temporary.

Expertise is no longer enough. This is the crucial difference faced by Generation Y, and indeed by all professionals seeking to compete in today's economy. This is the big change from the 1980s. No matter what your expertise is, there are now thousands more like you... or soon will be. And even if not, the relentless evolution of automation and commoditisation may well render any skill set redundant. Even yours. (Certainly ours.)

History abounds with examples, particularly since the Industrial Revolution. However, this is not a book about history, nor about economics; you may need to read about these forces elsewhere. The book *is* about the behaviour change needed to cultivate opportunity, and most importantly developing the *courage* to make that change.

So what is currently happening? How are people responding to the need for new jobs, new markets, new opportunities?

Networking frenzy

Since the Millennium, there has been a huge emphasis on networking and relationship building in business. This networking frenzy has now moved online, particularly into social media. Every day is about making connections; then getting key messages across to the people you meet. Professionals are starting to think about their 'social capital' as much as their 'intellectual' or 'financial' capital. Books have been written about this, and new tools such as video and smartphones constantly create new potential for 'connecting'.

But when everyone is broadcasting 'messages', who is being heard?

At the same time, decision-makers at every level occupy their current roles for shorter and shorter periods of time. Often, by the time you have cultivated the relationship, the buyers have moved on. If they are actively networking at all, it's usually with their *own* future very much in mind.

Then, when opportunities do come by, there is a bewildering array of options open to the purchaser. So many options that they sometimes make no purchase at all; and instead carry on lengthy dialogues with potential suppliers, employees and advisers. Or just as you get to the final hurdle... someone 'above' changes the plan and that tasty job or contract disappears overnight.

When a professional starts to wake up to the need for opportunity, they usually become very busy. They start connecting online, and begin to send out more emails than ever before. They go into 'broadcast mode': making offers, running events, starting discussion groups and/or charity bike-rides. Up until then you couldn't get hold of them; now all of a sudden they are calling you. Or they start seeking courses and qualifications, in the long-cherished belief that more expertise will create more opportunity.

The truth is that the vast majority *are ill-prepared for the world in which they find themselves*. They developed their careers in a different economy, where education and expertise were passports to prosperity. When certain skills were no longer required by the marketplace (as happened to programmers with COBOL, art directors with Letraset and joiners when boat-builders moved from wood to fibre-glass), the solution might not have been easy, but at least it was straightforward: develop another set of expertise that is in demand. Or else downsize and take early retirement, living off equity and investments. If you were lucky enough to have equity and investments, of course.

The majority have no choice but to start connecting or start learning: usually both. In this book, it is not our purpose to disparage these worthy activities; they are important to the ability to stay relevant and create opportunity.

But something more is usually needed.

Why 'cultivating' opportunity?

When it comes to creating new openings and opportunities, where can Adam look for some assistance? For the business owner or divisional manager responsible for opportunity and business growth, where do they look for strategy that is not out-of-date by the time they define it?

Skills and qualifications – even experience – are no longer in themselves sufficient as a passport to opportunity. As Adam is discovering, something more is required. And it's not just a problem for young jobseekers; it's also an issue for many seasoned IT developers, designers, accountants, technicians, lawyers, consultants, coaches, trainers and a host of managers with experience at every level.

Opportunities now have to be cultivated, not just discovered. This is a distinction that Adam's college teachers have not yet imparted to Adam for the simple reason that they themselves are products of the expertise economy, and their mindset is still a knowledge (and skill) mindset.

Few professionals think about *cultivating* opportunity. All too often, their opening question is 'How can I/we help?' on the assumption that the opportunity already exists, and simply has to be discovered. Consultants even talk about 'requirements gathering', as if the requirements were already there, growing on the trees like ripe fruit, and just had to be picked.

In many ways, the expertise economy resembled a 'hunter-gatherer' forest where, as long as you had the skills to shoot arrows, there was opportunity enough for everyone. But now that everyone is qualified in archery, we all need to evolve. Something like an agricultural revolution is needed, to feed the millions in search of work across the globe. The capacity to cultivate opportunity requires more than learned expertise. It requires more than intellectual ability, too.

It certainly requires courage.

In the economy of the future, we can all expect to be playing a more active part in opening up new opportunities. It will not be as simple as responding to an advertisement, or waiting to be called for an interview. The challenge of creating opportunity will be there both for individuals and for entire enterprises.

This is the context in which 'the courage to ask' is important. For example, we can expect to see the following shifts:

From	To
Responding to job advertisements	Proactively contacting organisations regarding new research or initiatives
Writing proposals and tenders	Collaborating pre-proposal, providing some value up-front
Inventing new services for customers	Close collaboration with key customers, developing services with them vs for them
Updating my CV	Short video case studies, consisting of client interviews and featuring results

The good news is that a busy hive of opportunity creation will in turn create new needs and new potential. Today we spend money to fulfil needs that our grandparents never imagined. Just as your granny didn't need a personal-image consultant, and Grandad wasn't agonising over software platforms, we can all expect new services and needs to emerge. Equally, we can expect to play a part in that evolution: not just to wait for it.

Furthermore, the ability to cultivate opportunity should not be confused with the skill to cultivate relationships. While the latter skill is certainly useful, thousands of great relationship builders are now out of work. If Adam just starts calling up his friends and asking, 'How are you?', he may well enhance his sense of connection with his old mates from college; but he may equally find that some are very busy and, as a result, Adam may feel neglected or even ignored. There has to be a better reason for that phone call.

This book is about *one single ability* needed to cultivate opportunity: the *'courage to ask'*. This ability is, however, a prerequisite for many of the other skills in opportunity creation. For example, there is no point in coming up with an innovative idea if you cannot go on to create the opportunity within which this great idea has value. Or, at the very least, partner-up with someone who has the capability to do just that. As we will see later on, partnership is a very viable form of opportunity creation, but partnership too starts with the *'courage to ask'*.

Asking is where influence begins. Without the courage to ask, much skill development is wasted, and may even be a recipe for frustration, disappointment and debt.

Viewed in this way, you would imagine that most people would be eager to develop their 'asking abilities'. In practice, however, this is not always the case.

Resistance

First, a question for you: If you were Adam, at the end of that last chapter, would you have gone for a run? Did you go for a run? Or would you have turned the page?

Knowing what to do, deciding to do something and doing it... these are all very different things.

Most people turn the page (but recommend that Adam go for a run). Even those who are hungry for lunch want to check if the book is worth coming back to after lunch. Perhaps you are reading this on a train, so you tell yourself that you would have gone for a run if you were at home.

It's easier to keep reading than to do something. Without doubt, some self-help books have inspired some people to change some aspect of their lives. But the majority of books serve to *postpone* change, simply by giving the reader another book to read. Maybe they should be called 'self-hinder' books: it's perhaps more accurate.

Sure, it's easier to read another chapter than to go for a run. It's easier to replan the to-do list than to action some of the items on it. No matter what strategy a book contains, the first experience that Adam will have is *resistance*.

Once again, Adam is not alone. *Most people resist the challenge of cultivating opportunity.* No matter how experienced or senior they are, the majority of professional people would rather delegate the responsibility for opening up opportunities to somebody else. They can explain this in countless convincing ways: perhaps their lack of time or by telling you that their talents lie elsewhere.

These explanations always have a certain plausibility. There is always something else to do first. When companies are in crisis, they would rather change the organisation, even do painful cutbacks, chop bonuses or away-days... *anything* other than confront the challenge of *creating opportunity* **with** *their customers*. When individuals are in crisis, they would rather blame the boss or the economy, stay in bed, do a course, or reformat their CV (yet again) than start the scary process of asking questions of others, and making requests of them.

Here's a classic example: John did some mentoring work with a video-production company that went on to successfully reposition itself in a tough B2B market. Part of their revised offer was to create innovative videos with clients, featuring *the client's* customers in very stylish ways. For example, they might make an impressive video with a clothing retailer featuring young shoppers, and the shoppers would in turn share the video on social media. Free, viral promotion, which seems to work as long as the video follows a certain 'recipe'.

Because they have considerable experience of doing these videos, this video-production company has convincing success in this area, along with a long list of classic pitfalls into which most organisations fall when they try to do this on their own. So when they propose making a video (with a clothing retailer or hotel, for example), what is the number one problem they encounter?

Money? No, the investment is not huge. Time? No, they can usually do all the filming in a day, and the post-production within a week. Risk? Hardly, the investment is low and the client always controls the finished product.

The number one problem is that deep down most organisations are *afraid of the relationship with their customer*. When it comes right down to it, the store will *resist* asking the young shopper to get involved. They experience the same phenomenon of *resistance* that Adam experienced when it came to going for a run, which a professional experiences when contemplating asking for referrals, which a sensitive manager experiences when they prepare to ask a team member to 'raise their game'.

Sometimes, this *resistance* will be quite sophisticated. Even experienced, successful professionals will tell you about phone calls they avoid, tasks they delay and conversations they have postponed. When they trust you enough, they will start to confess some of the ways in which they hide this problem from themselves, that is, their techniques of *sophisticated procrastination.*

Here's our 'Top Ten'. There are plenty more from which to choose, but we don't want to be accused of giving you any fresh ideas in this area...

1. **Preparation** This is particularly sophisticated because of course we are never prepared enough. So preparation is 'justified'. There is always something else to research or to check. Perhaps we need another level of approval? Or more data?

2. **Strategising** It's easier to amend the strategy than to get on with it and test results. For example, it's easier for a clothing retailer to have another meeting about using social media than to make an inexpensive video with a few young shoppers and see what happens.

3. **Delegation** When a courageous conversation is needed, there are often good reasons why we suddenly need to focus on something else. Hutchinson's Law: 'If a situation requires undivided attention, it will occur simultaneously with a compelling distraction.' So we can then delegate that unpleasant task to someone else – for example, the store manager – who in turn will find their own reason to resist, or something else that is higher priority.

4. **Systems and Infrastructure** Adam would probably find it more appealing to upgrade his PC or change his database, than to talk to some of the people in it. Don't entire companies do the same?

5. **Revisiting Purpose, Vision or Mission** Adam may well respond, 'I don't see how going for a run will help me find a job.' In fairness, he has a point: more about this later. For now, just notice how the feeling of resistance *precedes* the intellectual explanation that follows. For many analytical professionals, it is more attractive to revisit *why* they are doing something, rather than actually getting on and doing it.

6. **Perfecting** and fine-tuning documents, CVs, proposals, presentations, emails, etc., rather than picking up the phone and asking a question.

7. **Messaging** Given Generation Y's appetite for emails, texts and Facebook updates, this is growing in significance. There is always a host of messages to respond to, and an uneasy feeling often accompanies not being 'plugged in'. Message-and-response provides an unlimited cover story for being busy.

8. **Analysis** Comparing youth-unemployment figures in different countries, and/or arguing if Germany has a better system... economics and politics can provide anyone with a near-perfect smokescreen for not doing anything about their own situation. Just Google 'youth employment' for the evidence of this. Can you see some practical solutions in all that commentary, solutions that Adam could apply? Usually not. The commentators are so busy comparing figures and theorising about causes, there is little time left for practical solutions.

9. **Google** Any of us can fill our days following the information trails that lead from one little box on a screen. Add YouTube, email, LinkedIn (plus several more platforms that will emerge before you finish this book) and you may even forget to have lunch.

10. **Reorganising** themselves ...yet again. It's often more interesting than actually doing something.

Notice how all the Top Ten are worthy activities in their own right. We're not just talking about watching afternoon TV, blatant laziness or staring out the window. Entire books are written about planning and research, so these activities provide a perfect smokescreen to hide the things we avoid doing.

Even a crisis is not enough to catapult many people into proactive creation of opportunity. The courage to ask is elusive. And ask what, you might ask? Just who are we asking, and what are we asking for?

This book will deal with these questions thoroughly, but first let's take a trip to Paris and meet someone very different to Adam, but who is also in need of new approaches, new questions and new solutions.

4

Paris High Rise (Janique)

*'Courage doesn't always roar. Sometimes courage
is the little voice at the end of the day that says
"I'll try again tomorrow"'* – *Mary Anne Radmacher*

It's 7am and the January sun casts long shadows across the Paris
suburb of Le Raincy. In her 12th floor apartment, Janique is
preparing breakfast for her two children and herself, in preparation
for a long day ahead. The smell of coffee mingles with the squeals
of *Oui Oui* on TV, before which her youngest daughter sits in rapt
attention.

Janique could be described as one of France's *Nouveaux
Pauvres* (New Poor). Five years ago, she was married and living in a
large house in the chic surrounding of the 16e arrondissement. Her
professional life was accelerating: she was a marketing manager for
a consulting organisation and, between her and her husband, their
combined take-home salaries allowed for frequent holidays and a
lifestyle they were both proud of.

But the economic crisis brought redundancy, and in turn family
crisis. Janique and her husband fought an acrimonious divorce;
and in parallel both lost their jobs for separate unrelated reasons.
The house had to be hurriedly sold at a loss, and they ended up
owing money to the bank, including enormous legal fees following
the bitterly disputed divorce.

People said Janique was courageous, but she believes she acted
out of necessity. As the abyss opened up around her, she decided to
cut her losses and move to a location that was affordable and that
provided an easy commute to the centre of Paris. Rents in Le Raincy

were cheap, particularly in the wake of the riots in neighbouring Clichy-sous-Bois a few years earlier.

The move was a big change for Janique and her children. In eighteen months, they lost their father, their house, their garden, their friends and easy access to everything they needed. They moved to this 'HLM' high-rise block (low rent) where they now live on a tight budget. Their father has not visited in six months; the last Janique heard of him he was in hospital for depression.

'I am so completely on my own, it's hard to describe. Every hour of every day is spent in the battle for survival. I found work as a secretary but my total net pay is 1,655 euros per month, and this has to meet our every expense. All our food and clothes are bought in markets that I didn't even know existed until recently.

'Sometimes I wonder if my former life was real. Did I really flash my credit card in restaurants, often without even glancing at the bill? Was it really us that went on holiday to Costa Rica, the Maldives and the Seychelles? Now I have to save up to put petrol in our little Peugeot: the last vestige of our middle-class life.

'People say "Don't give up" and I don't. I can honestly say that I have applied for every marketing job that has come up for the past five years, irrespective of location. Late into every night, after the children go to bed, I draft another ten emails, customise another ten CVs and send out another ten letters. I don't allow myself to go to bed until I have done ten. Sometimes, that's very late indeed.

'The response is always the same. Recruitment agents explain that every marketing manager job gets at least a hundred applications, and now they are looking for specialist experience such as social media campaigns and repositioning of brands. Given that I'm nearly five years out of that workplace, my skills are starting to age, and I seriously doubt that I could do that job today.

'Anyway, on some days I'm happy enough with my secretarial job. It pays the bills and my boss is nice. But it frustrates me when I think of all that study, all that potential; that I'm capable of so much more. And I feel guilty that I cannot give more to my children: this is not the environment in which I wanted to raise them.

'Yet I'm kept going by the thought that I'm honestly doing the best I can for them. No matter how long the days, I feel I am doing the most important job in the world, that of being a good mother. I keep going because of them and to me that is important. I feel like Cinderella, cheering up her long days of endless chores by talking to the birds. There is love in our little home and this has kept us together.

'Any form of further education or retraining is out of the question: I have neither the time nor the money. I have thought of doing a course on Saturdays, but who would look after the children? And when would I do the course work? Plus everything costs money; and then what's the guarantee at the end? I read about many graduates like me without work.

'No matter which way I turn, every door seems to be closed. So I focus on what I can do: I can be grateful that I have my little job, my children are healthy and that so far nothing bad has happened in our immediate neighbourhood.

'I laugh when I look back at some of the books I bought on self-development. With hindsight, they all seem to be the self-indulgent luxuries of another decade: together with shoe shops on the Champs Elysées or holidays in Costa Rica. If it were just me, I know I can do without these things. But then I look at my children, and their future... and that's another story.'

The New Poor

In France alone, there are an estimated two million people like Janique: living just above the official poverty line, unsupported by social security or unemployment benefits. In many cases, the Nouveaux Pauvres come from comfortable backgrounds, with university degrees, literate and articulate, well-travelled. Many are retired, but for a variety of reasons, their pensions have not kept pace with rising costs of living. There are many formerly middle-class people of all ages, some aged eighty-plus, whose days are spent in the battle for survival.

If you listen to them, you will certainly hear about money: the weekly battle to make ends meet. But there are two other things that are equally important. For many the lack of **time** is a more serious handicap than lack of money. By the time Janique has attended to her job, her children, her shopping and her job applications, there is just no time left for play or development. If she had more time (and energy) she might be able to find a way out of the impasse.

This creates the second issue: **isolation**. Janique feels so alone with her pain and her sense of failure. There are no friends popping by, and even if there were, Janique has little time to receive them. The cocktail parties, social groups, evening classes and all the ways that Janique might meet others all cost money. As often happens with stress, divorce and relocation, friends get lost along the way.

Effort

'It's now after midnight, and the children are asleep. I have sent my ten CVs, tidied away the toys and emptied the school-bags. This evening I watched a programme on FR3 that says that there are over two million of us: this worries me even more. I feel I am in prison, and my energy is so low. I am feeling my way around the walls, searching for a door. There has to be a door somewhere and there has to be a way to open it.'

Without any doubt, Janique is working harder than Adam. With sole responsibility for two children, no parents to make her lunch, already in debt, her life is one of *boulot, métro, dodo* (work, commute, sleep). Unlike Adam, Janique is in employment, but this means she is now caught by time poverty as well as money poverty. Furthermore, she is experiencing 'friend poverty', and as we will see later on, this is having a huge effect on her courage.

Somehow, however, Janique keeps going. She believes that there has to be a 'door somewhere'. Despite the terrible trap in which she is caught, her love for her children is sustaining her.

Asking

Despite all the obvious differences, there are some important similarities between Janique and Adam. *Neither is asking: neither is making requests.* Each is broadcasting in their own way, both are sending off CVs. Each of them is demonstrating a rugged determination. Both are scouring online job-boards. Unfortunately for them, so are thousands of others.

Both Adam and Janique are using Google: that's about as far as their 'asking' takes them. OK, Adam has popped a few 'asks' into his Facebook status update. Janique has probably sent an occasional email asking about whom her CV should be sent to. But if either of them were to start logging the requests they were making on a daily basis, what would they find?

Discomfort

Professionals in all walks of life are uncomfortable with requests. There is something about 'asking' that feels awkward. This phenomenon is not confined to jobseekers: we will see shortly that experienced employed professionals also fear making requests of their clients and colleagues. Managers are equally anxious about asking certain questions of team members and many would rather find another approach that didn't involve *asking*.

Yet *asking* is vital. Without the ability to make requests and pose certain questions, the ability to create opportunity is limited. Without the ability to make requests, we cannot engage the help that we need.

So why is asking so difficult? Is it simply that Adam and Janique do not perceive the importance of *asking*, or is there more to it?

We believe there is *much* more to it, and that's what this book is about. Until we understand this properly, any so-called 'solutions' will simply add to Adam's and Janique's disappointment with themselves. There are thousands of jobseeking guides and sales courses that specify great questions to ask. But the problem lies not in the *question*; the problem lies in the *asking*.

When it comes to making requests or posing questions, we are usually swimming against the tide. With prospective customers and employers, we can expect resistance. Most importantly, we create resistance ourselves. Both our culture and our psychology tend to sabotage our efforts before we even get started to create opportunity. For example, we might think 'I am not entitled to approach this person', 'They are too busy', or 'I'm sure they have thought of this already'.

This is true even when professionals think they have no problem with asking. Many confident professionals and managers will tell you that they are 'asking' every day. But what are they asking? How are they doing so? Adam thinks he's asking with his occasional Facebook updates... but is he? And what opportunity is that asking creating?

Asking is uncomfortable. No matter how much we believe

in the value of asking, a host of forces – cultural, psychological, tactical and behavioural – will often conspire to distract us via 'sophisticated procrastination'.

Exercise

What requests do you make? What opportunity do those requests cultivate?

As the first of a few simple exercises to really bring this to life try logging the requests you are making (and separately, wanting to make) on a sheet of paper. Keep a daily record for a week. At the end of the week try grouping them into themes and give each theme a name. What sort of requests are you making? In what volumes? What requests do you want to make but don't? Why? What opportunity are you accessing by making each of those requests – that is, what do people do as a consequence of your asking?

If you are honest with yourself, you may discover a big chunk of truth about your access to opportunity.

5
Karl the Confident

*'The meeting of preparation with opportunity generates
the offspring we call luck' – Tony Robbins*

A successful programme manager in the Netherlands, Karl will tell
you he has no problem with asking. Indeed, it's his job. Every day,
he is asking the questions that other project managers and business
analysts are not asking.

When Karl sits down with an end-user manager or systems
developer, he's not just listening to what they are saying, he's also
wondering about what they are *not* talking about. What have they
not taken into consideration? What could go wrong here? Why
are they doing it this way? How is this contributing to the overall
programme? Whose support will be needed next?

Karl is not afraid of questions. Neither is he afraid of making
requests. 'Next time we meet, can you show me...' 'Before we start
spending money on this, can you first check the assumption that...'
'May I ask that you treat this deadline as non-negotiable?' These
are words that people like Karl have to articulate every day.

As in many business cultures, Karl inhabits a world where it
does not pay to appear uncertain. If you don't know what you want
to explore, please don't waste my time! So, not surprisingly, Karl
will probably be wondering if we're not just making a lot of fuss
about nothing. You just build your confidence, and get on with it,
right? That's what Adam has to learn. And the best way to learn this
is to do it. Next!

Having worked with many Karls – in organisations large and
small – we observe that they are exceedingly confident *within the*

context of their role. In other words, while there is an abundance of opportunity for Karl to exercise his programme-management skills, he will have no trouble asking questions and making requests. As he says, it's his job. It's what he does.

But if Karl is taken *outside* his programme-management role, into the uncertain space of opportunity development, for example, an entirely different pattern of behaviour occurs. Let's now fast-forward the clock a couple of years and see what this looks like.

Karl still appears active and dynamic; now his daily activities consist of sending messages, doing calls, broadcasting invitations, setting up meetings, renewing old relationships, giving talks, proposing alliances, doing research, analysing data, sending emails… indeed just about everything other than making requests.

What has happened to Karl the Confident? Let's hear it from him, directly.

Straight talking

'Here in the Netherlands, we are direct. We tell it as it is. We don't beat around the bush.

'The last two years have been tough. Our customers, both in healthcare and consumer goods, started cutting back on projects, so two of us were freed up from our programme-management roles to develop new opportunities. Though we've certainly had some success, unfortunately it's not as much as our senior management would like.

'Yes, I'm apprehensive about what comes next. I will be forty-five later this year, with two kids in college. I am the sole income earner in my family. The opportunities for senior programme managers are finite, and the competition intensifies by the month as more programme-management skill comes onto the market.

'I'm also frustrated. We have done *everything* to create opportunity: quality events, thought-leadership initiatives, social media, market research, referral programmes, associates, alliances… you name it, we've done it. I'm coming to the conclusion that the projects we want just don't exist.

'Don't talk to me about asking! I've asked for meetings, I've followed up consistently, I've requested introductions and referrals. I honestly don't believe that we have been defective in this regard.

'Winning business is about demonstrating credibility, and providing evidence of that credibility. People want to know what we have done, and the results we have produced. We are a straight-talking country; when you are granted a meeting, you have to come straight to the point and state what you are offering. We just don't have time for questions that beat around the bush.'

Frustration

Karl's frustration is palpable, and his mood is unlikely to accommodate fresh suggestions right now. Furthermore, he is fatigued as well as frustrated. Imagine you are in his shoes: you've had a successful career, with a straight growth trajectory for about twenty years, and then – precisely because of your success – you are made responsible for developing opportunities which are not materialising. Just at that moment in history when the tectonic plates shift and there are economic earthquakes, changes and uncertainties everywhere.

Karl does everything he knows. He works harder than ever. He gets up earlier and makes phone calls. He sets up meetings and gives presentations about the benefits of good programme management. He gets back in touch with former clients. He initiates discussions on social media, and uses every spare moment to respond and comment. Late in the evening, he writes proposals and tender documents. And he networks and invites people to his events.

After two years of this, and disappointing results, Karl is understandably fatigued and apprehensive. And he probably doesn't want to be told that there is something he hasn't tried. Particularly when he believes it conflicts with his culture, with how things 'should be done'.

The culture factor

Karl has certain beliefs about how a business meeting should be run. These beliefs are in part a product of his culture. There are many other parts, too: his professional upbringing, his family, and so forth. Culture may be roughly described as 'the way we do things around here'.

Our cultural lenses play a significant part in how we see the world. Most people only become aware of this when they have some experience outside their home turf. For now, let us just note that the Netherlands is indeed a very direct culture, where you get to the point quickly, you make your request and it gets answered equally directly. Yes means Yes and No means No. Contrast this with the UK, for example, where 'Yes, we want to do that' is often a precursor to telling you why they don't want to do it. In the Netherlands, if they don't want to do something, they just tell you.

Therefore, when Karl goes into a meeting, he is expected to state why he is there, provide succinct evidence of their achievements, and make his pitch without too much preamble.

So far, so good. But let's face it, Karl's approach is not working: it's not cultivating opportunity. So why not try something else, *even if it is countercultural?*

When it comes to cultivating opportunity via requests and questions, the culture is often against you. In hierarchical cultures (for example, France, Malaysia, Spain) you may not feel entitled to talk to certain people, far less make requests of them. In low-context, direct cultures (for example, Germany, Netherlands, Denmark), you may feel obliged to go straight into pitch-mode. In high-context, indirect cultures (Southern Europe, Japan, Ireland) the relationship-build may take so much energy that it's hard to make a direct request at all.

In terms of asking, the UK presents an interesting paradox. On the one hand the culture is highly individualist and success driven. There is a high tolerance of uncertainty coupled with low 'power distance' (that is, a belief that inequalities between people should be minimised). All these factors favour an 'asking culture'. At the same time, there is that legendary British modesty and a talent for understatement: what is said is not always what is meant. You have to read between the lines, which can be very confusing for foreigners trying to open up opportunity in the UK.

Even in favourable climates, asking often feels like swimming against the cultural current. When we ask a question, or make a request, there is always the risk that we won't like the answer. Furthermore, the question and/or request may be 'inappropriate'. For example, it is not acceptable in most Asian cultures to embarrass someone by obliging them to say No. There is simply no point in asking, 'Do you understand what I'm asking you to do?'; yet this mistake is made by Westerners in Asia all the time.

So should we just ignore the culture? Certainly not. Whether we like it or not, it's operating all around us. Furthermore, if we try to ignore the culture, or simply acknowledge it without really understanding how it's operating, our ability to influence diminishes. Put another way, if we ignore the current, we just get carried away by it.

In a sense, that's exactly what's happening to Karl. If he were really confident, why not swim *across the cultural current*, rather than just go with the flow of its expectations about how a meeting should run? For example, rather than starting with a message or a presentation, what if he turned the entire meeting into a *request*? Something that would take him closer to his customer's world, and their real needs?

Even if this challenged the norm. For example, Karl might say...

> *'Before we get into today's agenda, can I just ask one question?'*
> *'Happy to share what we've being doing with x; before doing so, can I just ask...?'*
> *'Of all the challenges you are facing, why is this top of the agenda?'*

Taking this further, Karl might propose a study, doing some benchmarking, or committing some investigation resource to an as-yet unresolved question in the customer's mind. In short, something that's about *them*, not about him and programme management.

Why should Karl do so? This will be a question that the customer will also ask. In the Netherlands, we can expect it to be asked quite directly. 'Why are you investing this time and energy?' Karl will need to have his answer ready.

He will need courage, too. If Karl is going to swim across the current, he will need to be willing to take risks in dialogue.

Facing the challenge

Many people like Karl are currently rethinking how they get business. Some have noticed a changing climate, and are adapting to it before they are forced to do so. Others are just ignoring the issue, or making it someone else's problem. Still others are waiting for an upturn: a rising tide that will lift all boats. Unfortunately for them, waiting is dangerous. Like that (not-so-old) Chinese proverb: 'Man who stand on hill with mouth wide open... He wait long time for roast duck to fly in.'

There are also those who dismiss opportunity creation as 'just a selling problem', and who would prefer to deal with some other, less risky, more familiar leadership challenge: for example, yet another reorganisation. We have already discussed this particularly sophisticated form of procrastination in Chapter 3.

If Karl has been struggling with a lack of opportunity for two years, time may be running out; both for him and for his organisation. Making Karl redundant may reduce their costs, but it still won't increase their sales. If opportunity is not being created, companies will close fewer deals, which means less revenue, more redundancy and fewer resources for investment and reward. Opportunity is like oxygen: if the air is too thin, our ability to perform is weakened – no matter how fit we were beforehand.

The challenges that Karl is facing are in many ways different to those faced by Adam and Janique. They would both regard Karl as privileged. He still has resources available that they don't have (support, colleagues, training, success stories, time). He has experience and credibility. Though a bit anxious, his confidence is still intact. He has a network from which he can create meetings.

Yet Karl has more to lose. At some level, he is aware of that, too. He senses that there is a rollercoaster ride ahead. Janique has already been through the shock descent that awaits many people in today's middle class. Karl is vaguely aware that the same fate may befall anyone – even him.

Uncertainty

There is another important factor at work here: partly cultural and partly psychological. Karl's entire background has a *low tolerance for uncertainty*. His work as a programme manager is that of *conquering* uncertainty, by envisaging risks and countering them beforehand. When one is managing projects, designing systems, drafting agreements or drawing up forecasts... uncertainty is never good news.

A distaste for uncertainty is characteristic of most professions, and this is further accentuated in the Netherlands which scores high on cultural indexes of 'Uncertainty avoidance'. In this context, ambiguity brings anxiety, and there is an emotional need for 'rules': whether these rules are seen to work or not.

In professional life, the attitude to uncertainty is to 'colonise' it as quickly as possible, and to impose controls, procedures, reviews and agreements in order to protect us from its chaotic attacks. In short, we prefer to deal in *answers* rather than in open *questions*. When a question is posed, we start structuring the response as quickly as possible. For example, we start specifying the dimensions of the problem, or the scope of our enquiry, rather than live with the question.

Furthermore, we start projecting this intolerance of uncertainty onto others. So we naturally assume that they too want answers, not more questions. We assume that their purpose in meeting us is to 'tell them the answer' to their problems, or to hear us present this to them. Assuming that such a presentation will establish our credibility, we go into 'presentation mode' early on, whether they have invited us to do so or not.

Karl may reply that he does not do this, that the purpose of the meeting is to present his company's services. But who defined that agenda? And even if the customer did ask for a presentation, did Karl first attempt a request that they initially do something else?

Probably not. It takes courage to say, 'I can certainly give you a brief overview of what we do, but what we would most like to do next Thursday is to share experience on the challenges of x; is that OK?'

The ability to create opportunity is enhanced by being able to live with a *question* – and get others involved in that question – rather than trying to sell your *answers*. If Karl can marshal enough energy to shift his dialogue a bit, some of these brick walls may start coming down.

Courage

Doing things that are countercultural is never easy. Taking meetings in a different direction to what the client is expecting, challenging the indecisive manager to make up his mind, refusing to drop the rate any further, persisting in a line of questioning that produces quizzical looks... this all takes courage.

This approach has its pitfalls too: the risk of appearing arrogant is certainly one of them. As the famous architect Frank Lloyd Wright once said, 'Early in life I had to choose between honest arrogance and hypocritical humility; I chose honest arrogance and have seen no occasion to change my mind.' It takes real courage to set aside what others think of you, and to ask that courageous question anyway.

It's particularly difficult when there is a whole culture against you. If you are in a law firm you may be surrounded by the culture of the hourly rate, where every six minutes has significance. A financially run organisation may be a culture of numbers. A sales-led organisation may be so obsessed by end-of-month targets, that it has no time for real opportunity creation. An academic organisation may be obsessed by who publishes first or course numbers.

On top of that, everyone is busy with something else. Whether this is reorganisation, infrastructure, strategy, planning, product development or delivery of current business, there is a host of reasons for sophisticated procrastination. Anyone can invoke culture to explain lack of results.

In addition, it is more appealing to deal in answers than in questions. When we are in our area of expertise, we are in our comfort zone. It should now be evident that, when it comes to 'the courage to ask', there are many forces operating against us. Naturally, you will be getting impatient to get your teeth into some solutions.

But we are not finished yet. Our request of you is to rest with the discomfort and impatience, as there are some more layers of the onion to peel. The difficulty with asking also applies even to those senior managers with whom Karl is dealing. Let's meet one of them.

6

Maria in the Air

'Courage is resistance to fear, mastery of fear
– not absence of fear' – Mark Twain

'As I fly back from Kuala Lumpur, I wonder how long I can keep this up. This is my third long-distance flight this month, but at least it's one of the few times I get to concentrate without interruption.

'My organisation is one you will know of. If you are reading this online, you are probably using our technology along the way. With offices in every country of the world, we have a complicated regional and divisional structure. I am the HR Director for a global division, and that's as much as I am willing to tell you.

'I know about 'resilience', 'human capital', 'talent management' and 'employee engagement': it's my job. It's been my job for the past twelve years, via a variety of roles and organisations. We live in a fast-moving world, where careers evolve in months rather than in years. There is little time for history.

'So I am writing about the present, and the very near future. To all appearances, I am a success. I am the head of a global division in a respected international organisation. My salary and benefits, taken together, are higher than most people dream about. At work, I have a team to take care of detailed implementation. At home, I can afford any level of domestic support I need. My husband works from home, and he takes care of all that. Our financial advisers assure us our investments are doing well, so even if I were a casualty of some future reshuffle we would be OK. Probably. Who knows for sure, these days?

'So… why do I feel like this?

'It's difficult to explain. Something is wrong, and I cannot put my finger on it. There is never enough time to figure it out. When I get off this flight, there will be more messages needing reply, meetings and webex's in need of rescheduling, my daughter whom I have not seen all week, and my mother who has Alzheimer's. There is no time for self-indulgence.

'Just before catching this flight, I travelled with Bob to the airport. He confided in me that on Tuesday next, they will be deciding a level of headcount reduction, plus the possible closure of certain offices. He wants me in the US next week to start planning the announcements, and to decide how we transfer competencies. How do I now fit this in? Yet how can I *not* be involved in these decisions?

'I'm trying not to think about that. These few hours are *for me* and I want to try and figure out what's wrong before we land at Heathrow. Because something is certainly wrong. Physically, I feel OK, apart from occasional headaches and tiredness. But I'm mentally and emotionally exhausted, and I can no longer find any sense in what I'm doing.

'On two occasions in the past six weeks, I came within a hair's breadth of resigning. Sure, I know it's crazy to make impulsive decisions like that, and I'm glad I didn't. But I cannot ignore this voice of inner necessity. Something is wrong; what is it?

'OK. Stocktake. Now aged forty-one. Top of class in school, first-class hons from university, recruited by top consulting firm. Worked flat out, played the game, built my network. Specialised in talent management, ahead of the curve. Headhunted at twenty-six – good God, that was fifteen years ago! Agh! Where have those months and years gone?

'But hang on, it's been fun and I've cleared quite a few hurdles along the way. I used to be nervous before presentations in front of senior people; now it does not cost me a thought. With each role came more credibility and soon I was being invited to present on talent management at conferences. Not that there was much time to go to these: there was enough to do already in the day job. But it was nice to be asked.

'I'm proud of a lot of the things we did. One of the reasons we are still growing is that we manage people well. We engage them not by asking for less; but by asking for more. We *involve* them and that takes more of their time but it also releases more of their value by return. And I have managed myself by the same standard, as well as those who work for me.

'But where does all of this end up? What's it all *for*? Year after year, doing more with less, getting results faster and faster: OK, now what? More importantly, for what?

'I feel so disconnected from the goals of my organisation. It's hard to write this down: I don't want to be that frustrated woman complaining about success in middle-age. Yet the truth is that it's hard to find people to talk to about this. The usual reaction from my female friends is, "Oh, give up the job, and take it easy. Why do you need to work like this?" But that's their life, not mine. I made my choices a long time ago, and giving up was not part of the plan.

'Others suggest I go independent, or join a niche consulting company. But I realise this is jumping out of the frying-pan and into the fire. We employ independents and I see what's happening out there. When I get back, I bet there will be another message from Karl and ten others, enquiring if we have yet made a decision about that programme. It must be tough for them. No thanks, I don't want their life either.

'For obvious reasons, I cannot share this issue at work. It would be incompatible with the role I am doing. My friends live in a different world. While waiting for flights, I occasionally browse the self-help sections of bookshops but the books tend to fall into two categories: either business books about achievement (some of which have been useful in the past but somehow not applicable to the issues I have now), or else they are 'downsizing books' about giving it all up, backpacking around Asia and doing yoga. I was never fond of backpacking and I prefer the gym to yoga.

'Has professional life always been so all or nothing? My father was a senior manager but I don't remember him working like this. There certainly were busy times, but he also had time for his golfing weekends. And he had a non-working spouse who kept the home running.

'But is it really the workload that's the issue? Or something else?

'I cannot say I am isolated. There is occasional loneliness but it's not the whole picture. My husband knows I am unhappy, he thinks it's fatigue. In part, David is right, but I'm convinced the fatigue is the product of something else; perhaps even several things. On this flight, that's what I want to identify.

'I guess I could find someone who would understand the space I am in, but what would I ask them? Or more likely, what would they ask me? If this was one of the managers at work, what would I say? We would probably have a conversation about values. Words like 'energy', 'innovation', 'achievement', 'excellence' and 'results' would appear on the whiteboard. Some scoring would be done on each word, and perhaps a bit of 'visioning' would follow.

'Then what?

'I look out the window; it's night over rural India. Below me is this vast country, and I'm sipping wine high overhead. Through the window, I look down at this huge brown expanse of land, where occasional lights twinkle like stars in an immense continent below. Little villages and towns... what are they thinking down there, tonight?

'What would it be like to live there? Surrounded by a large family, asleep. Just dreaming of today and tomorrow? Or worrying about a simple domestic problem?

'Now I'm crying because I know I can *never* be one of them. Neither in India nor in London, I will never be that average woman who is content with home and family. And tonight I wish I could be, but it's not going to happen. I made choices a long time ago and even if tomorrow I could give up everything and move to a little flat in suburbia, I would not be happy. That is a lonely admission to make.

'So here I am. As I am. Flying over India in the early hours of the morning. With a husband and a daughter and a big job and all the frantic mental activity that this creates. Monkey-mind, I think they call it down there. OK monkey, where do we go from here?'

Navigating choppy waters

Even by her own standards, Maria is a successful woman. Every day, she is interacting with confident, successful people. But even in the midst of frenetic interaction, success brings its own challenges. On the surface, there may be lots of connection, but most of this is at the level of role-play. It's interaction because of the *role* that Maria has, rather than because of *who* Maria is. And there is always an agenda. Or rather, multiple agendas behind every dialogue and meeting.

In the corporate marketplace, there is a culture among the 'Winners' and it's not a culture that tolerates uncertainty for very long. You are supposed to know what you are doing and why you are doing it. Those whose centre of gravity lies elsewhere tend to get filtered out. In the end, everyone is replaceable.

It's not easy to keep one's balance. Wave after wave of reorganisation has to be explained and a manager is often explaining the last wave when the next wave strikes. This means constant alertness, speed of adaptation, and incredible mental and physical stamina. Only those who are quick thinking, adaptable, able to manage both ambiguity and complexity can play at this level.

For many reasons, Maria cannot take her sense of 'something is wrong' to work. It would be perceived as weakness. Furthermore, her schedule does not leave much room for evening courses or random searches online. She is therefore stuck: experiencing difficulty even when trying to define what the problem is.

Different mindsets

Talking with friends is often touted as the solution to issues of motivation, but much depends on who the friends are. Maria has spent her life being purposeful and driven and so she gets a real buzz from achievement. Outside work, many of her personal friends have a different mindset, so when she shares her issues with them, they respond in terms that make sense for *them*, rather than for her.

People with money or health worries often have little sympathy for Maria. Yet her pain is just as real; perhaps even more so as it's less understood. The emptiness of success can be harder to explain than the terror of failure. Maria is struggling *both* with the question to ask, as well as finding the right environment to start asking it.

It's not that Maria is isolated: unlike Janique she has many friends. But most people give feedback from where *they* are, rather than where Maria is. Maria knows this, and she is wary.

In her work you would imagine she has no problem making requests, but even senior leaders often find it easier to broadcast messages than to make requests. It's particularly hard to make a request when we are not sure what the request is. This can usually be done only with people that you really trust, and even then, it takes real courage to ask.

Let's assume, however, that if Maria searches enough, sooner or later she will meet someone who understands her mindset and also the world in which she operates. Hopefully, someone who does not have their own agenda, or who is not just trying to profit from Maria's unhappiness and frustration. As Maria knows, that happens, too.

Will Maria have the courage to ask for support? We know she can confidently make requests at work, but will she have the courage to say, 'Something is wrong and I don't know what it is'? Will she trust the other person enough for a dialogue to be meaningful?

In the previous chapters, we have seen how easily sophisticated procrastination can prevent a person from making requests of others. Even when we know the questions that we want to pose. If that is true, surely it's even more difficult to ask questions and make requests when we are uncertain what the question is.

In some ways, this is the greatest courage of all. As we have seen already, courage is only relevant in the presence of risk. When we find ourselves uncertain about those questions that we sense are deeply important to us though we don't know what they are; when there is no ready-made framework to start judging the answers; when we may meet with disapproval for asking the question: this is the space when courage often seems to be the only quality left.

Courageous questions

So what questions can Maria ask herself tonight? Only she can decide, but here are some examples:

- What really matters to me?
- If I achieve that objective, what does that give me? What does *that* give me? Etc.
- If my life were already ideal, how would I know?
- Beyond my role and responsibility, who am I?

Some people in Maria's situation have found the following

separation helpful, particularly when they manage a support function in a large organisation.

- Have to – To what extent are my tasks being imposed or demanded of me?
- Able to – To what extent do my tasks match my abilities (is my job too easy?)
- Want to – To what extent do my tasks correspond to what I really want...?

Even when a successful professional is not isolated, and has plenty of friends, it can be lonely at the top. While others sleep around her, Maria is tonight confronting significant questions of purpose and meaning on this long-haul flight. That takes courage. But, as we will see in Part Two, a sense of purpose and meaning is a gateway to courage, too.

7

The Shy Genius

'We either make ourselves miserable, or we make ourselves strong. The amount of work is the same'
– Carlos Casteneda

'Morning Hannah… coffee please.'

Without another word, Graham walks through to his office. Hannah observes him from the corner of her eye, as he pulls a file from his briefcase and plonks it on the big mahogany desk that is already piled high with papers.

Hannah has been Graham's secretary for over fifteen years, and she knows him well. Today, she reads all the signs of a hangover, and just hopes that it's an out-with-clients type of hangover. As opposed to a drinking-in-his-solitary-flat type of hangover, of which there has been a worrying increase in frequency over the past few months.

As the coffee brews, Hannah tries to remember the talented lawyer for whom she came to work so many years ago. Graham was always a bit of an introvert; for Hannah, that was part of his charm; along with his insatiable curiosity about the world, and the studied intensity with which he pursued his cases. She once described him to her friend Eileen as a 'shy genius', and she wondered if Eileen guessed the full extent of her attraction to her talented (and alas married) boss.

As she pours the coffee, Hannah breathes a quiet sigh of relief that she did not get involved. Graham had other affairs and they all ended badly. Despite his rotten time-keeping and complete disorganisation, women found him likeable. Few of them understood how little Graham cared for them; these affairs were just a part of his endless curiosity and craving for variety. Hannah wonders if the day would come when he would have his own regrets.

Graham does not even look up as she places the coffee on his desk, and Hannah notices that he's chewing his pencil and seems really worried today. She wonders if she should be worried too, as the practice has nose-dived since Graham's divorce last year.

Hannah does the accounts and can see revenue dropping fast. She reads the monthly profit and loss reports; probably more than Graham does, Hannah thinks anxiously. He has such a callous disregard for administration; as well as keeping appointments, financial control and anything that approaches order or tidiness. No wonder his wife left.

He's probably in debt. At least three clients are disputing his invoices, and the referrals seem to be drying up. Hannah wonders how much longer this can go on.

From bad to worse

Meanwhile, Graham stares at the file in front of him. One of his clients has made a complaint to the Law Society about the conduct of a recent property transaction. Graham is in more trouble than Hannah knows. He's aware that he should engage a really good colleague to defend him, but Graham is equally aware that he cannot afford it.

Things are going from bad to worse. He's behind with his rent, his payments to his ex, and the rent of the office premises. He's worrying how he can continue to employ Hannah, yet he knows he would be lost without her. In the office, she's his mother, protecting him from a hostile world.

He needs to get some new clients fast.

But prospecting for business takes energy, and Graham is feeling anything but energetic right now. On the contrary he is feeling a mixture of 'anxious' and 'depressed'. He wishes he hadn't opened that bottle last night; he promised himself that he wouldn't. What if he were becoming an alcoholic on top of all his other problems?

What's going on? The last few years have been tough: surely

life was not always like this? Thinking back, however, Graham remembers that he always had some degree of anxiety. Even as a student in law school, there was a constant anxiety as to whether he would get through the next exam. In some ways he needed that anxiety: he seemed to work better under pressure. He needed the adrenaline.

Adrenaline, buzz, a bit of excitement. Anything that took away the tedium of boring routine. Graham had hated school, but loved university. Law school was tough and challenging, but the drama society (and a succession of interesting girlfriends) allowed him to work hard, play hard and explore new frontiers.

So why is the adrenaline not working now? All Graham wants to do today is to go back to his flat and hide. It's taking all his energy to come into the office, knowing that Hannah is watching him all the time out of the corner of her eye.

God, how things had changed! When Hannah first arrived, it was great to have her around. He knew she placed him on a pedestal, and yes, he enjoyed that. It was great to have someone with whom to share his success. Unlike some of his peers, Graham was not flamboyant. Nevertheless, he had an appetite for recognition and admiration, and it was deeply satisfying to have even one attentive colleague with whom he could shine. How would he cope without her?

Graham sighs. Life's unfair. It's not as if he has not been trying. Even when working hard before the divorce, revenue was stubbornly stagnant. Some of the clients with big property transactions had disappeared in the economic crisis; fee pressure has forced renegotiation with others. His practice is fighting hard to retain its share of the local market.

Graham knows that something has to be done. Many in his profession are urging caution. Some are close to retirement age and don't wish to jeopardise the world that they know. Others are talking about the changing nature of the legal profession. Those who have lived through several upturns and downturns are suggesting that Graham knuckle down, look after every client and wait for the tide to turn.

But Graham is doubtful whether the firm is in tidal waters. Ideally, Graham would like to attract a younger, more dynamic level of clientele; businesses that are in growth rather than in decline.

Ideally, businesses that are on an acquisition trail, or international expansion, where Graham could perhaps be involved in more corporate financing and higher-value work, rather than the tedium of debt collection and residential conveyancing. God, that's so boring.

Going around in circles

As he chews his pencil, Graham feels fed-up. These problems have been going on for a couple of years now, and today finds him anxious, weary and depressed. Each time he tries to think of a way out, he finds himself going around in circles. Another month goes by. And now he has this Law Society complaint to deal with.

He chews his options along with his pencil. Perhaps he could acquire another practice, but he knows he hasn't the money to do so. And with his current overdraft, it's unlikely the bank will lend him enough. He could try something like sponsorship or PR, but these initiatives require both energy and money and there is no guarantee that this would produce the right result – nor even the right clients.

Graham asks himself where his current clients come from. Going through a few key names, he sees they usually come from referrals and recommendations: clients who have been content with his services and recommended the firm to other people. The problem, however, is that many B-clients tend to know other B-clients, so while referrals work well, it's not always bringing the clientele that Graham would ideally like to have.

So the work becomes dull, and Graham becomes bored, and clients become dissatisfied and end up making a complaint to the Law Society. Graham sighs again.

Between a rock and a hard place

Graham feels conflicted. On the one hand, he knows he should organise himself, put some energy into getting clients and all would eventually be well. He sees the wisdom of organic, steady growth: it's safer, less risky and a proven route to success. On the other hand, all this calls for more energy and work, and Graham still does not know how he is going to pay Hannah's salary next month.

As the pencil stub gets shorter, he tries to come at the problem via his own time management. Perhaps he could zone his diary a bit: get the 'substance work' done in the morning, and free up the afternoons for cultivating opportunity?

Then Graham remembers that that's exactly what he set out to do a year ago. So what happened? On some days, clients insisted on afternoon meetings so invariably his development time got sabotaged. Or lunches ran on a bit. OK, so that explained some of it, perhaps a couple of days per week. So what happened to the other days?

He goes back through his diary. Sure enough, he finds lunches with bank managers, accountants, and a couple of friends from larger legal firms. He also finds quite a few networking events, even an article that he started entitled 'The Future of Legal Services'. Graham feels a moment of relief when he finds proof that he has been proactive; but this is quickly followed by more frustration when he realises that all these efforts don't seem to have had the desired effect.

At various points over the past decade, Graham has consulted a variety of professionals who claimed they could help him grow his business. Crossing the room to the whiteboard, Graham starts to list the various initiatives he has tried to cultivate fresh opportunity, together with some of the roadblocks he has encountered:

- **Networking** Sometimes OK but: too many sellers, not enough buyers – wrong audience – time/energy consuming – boring people – costs money.
- **PR** – problems: expensive, hard to gauge results, brings more B-clients?
- **Blogging/Social media** Tried and gave up. More work. Unfamiliar. Does this really open doors for a lawyer?
- **Articles/Newsletter** Interesting to write, but what then?
- **Advertising** at train stations, etc. Costs £. More B-clients. Would probably have got them anyway via referral, without the spending.
- **Cold-calling** Hated it. Got fobbed off. Don't believe organisations buy legal services this way.
- **Speaking** Started but gave up. Couldn't get interesting events.
- **Partnership** with financial advisers/accountants/bank.

Limited success, but again many B-clients.
· **Search engine optimisation** do people hire lawyers this way?

Graham flops back in his chair, discouraged even before the day begins. Are his peers right? Should he just knuckle down and accept that this is it for the rest of his life: churning out agreements and mopping up the affairs of small-time businesses for ever-decreasing margins?

God, he needs more coffee. 'Hannah!...'

New markets

Whatever the problems in his personal life, Graham's business difficulties are shared by many organisations of all sizes. Right across the world, professional services are being commoditised by a combination of technology, globalisation and off-shoring. Existing markets are in decline, and new markets need to be found. Even when the time and resources are available, what exactly do professionals do, in order to find opportunity and reposition their services in higher-quality markets?

At this point, the marketeers and business consultants will usually have a field day telling Graham to define his target market, and build a nicely structured communications plan to reach them. No matter how well he has done it, they will tell him that he has not done it well enough. Getting the revised definition in place will no doubt cost him more time and more money. Money which Graham does not have.

But all of this begs the question: what then? Once he has defined a niche, a sector or a size of company, what does he do to cultivate opportunity there?

The PR experts will advocate PR; the communications specialists will advise him about his website and messaging, the Web gurus will talk about SEO optimisation and the social-media specialists will extol the virtues of LinkedIn. Graham has already discovered the Professional Theory of Relativity: the answer you get is relative to the expertise of the professional consulted, not the problem you are facing.

So Graham feels he is on his own. As he sips his coffee and nurses his hangover, he wonders how he can create opportunity... and soon. Being responsible for future opportunity is a lonely place to be. And as Hannah reappears with his second coffee, she's a living reminder that he needs to act fast.

A lonely role

Graham feels isolated in facing these challenges; even though there are many others facing the same problem. In many organisations and professional firms, large and small, experienced managers are suffering the same uncertainty and their difficulty is accentuated by the fact that professional colleagues and fellow managers are often adept at eschewing this area of responsibility, and making someone else responsible.

Business development is often perceived as high-risk responsibility. In good times, professionals can always get involved in deals that look certain, and in that way take a share of the credit. In tough times, there is someone to blame. Deep down, they know how hard it can be to cultivate opportunity, and so they seek safer responsibility elsewhere.

It seems that we all want new markets, but we would prefer it if someone else could find them for us.

Graham is still aware that he has a couple of options open to him. He can talk to professionals in other firms and see what they do. Obviously, he will need to be very selective about who he speaks to, avoiding, for example, competitors in his immediate area. He can also find an experienced business coach or mentor. But once again, he will have to find someone he can really trust: many advisers are all too adept at selling their own services and then reminding Graham that he is responsible for the results.

Getting out of broadcast mode

Being an introvert, Graham will be understandably reluctant to take his dilemma to others. Even if he does, there is a high likelihood that their solutions are also stuck in 'broadcast mode'. Just like Adam at the beginning of this book, the conventional way of marketing involves 'broadcasting your message'. While some certainly speak about the importance of cultivating relationships, the purpose of doing so is invariably to 'get your message across'.

If we look at the list on Graham's whiteboard, we can see that they all represent attempts to 'get his firm's message across'. While many professionals might advise Graham to refine his message, might it not be more worthwhile to step back from the whole 'messaging' model entirely?

Professionals like Graham tend to be good at intellectualising and creating the next 'big idea'. This is where his strengths lie. Accordingly, it makes double sense to step back from 'messaging': communication is always going to be that bit harder for introverts. Instead of worrying about the firm's message, why not instead focus on a new 'big idea'? Instead of going to market with a *message*, it's more useful for many professionals to go to market with a *question*. Not a pseudo-question, or a gimmick to get attention, or 'would you be interested in x?'; but a genuine question (or 'big idea') that engages the person who is asked.

But even if Graham has a set of superb questions, would he start asking, today? Would he continue to ask, until he got results?

One glance at Graham sipping his second coffee should be sufficient for us to know the answer. Right now, he has neither the energy nor the courage to initiate these conversations, nor to ask these questions. No matter how brilliant the questions, no matter how skilled he gets at asking them, the necessary power just isn't there.

Even while being down and upset, Graham will be very aware of his own negative feelings and lack of energy. Even though he is desperate for the rewards of opportunity, the energy to take even the smallest steps in that direction somehow cannot be found.

So before Graham can deal with any 'asking', he will first have to deal with the 'courage to ask'.

8
Cultural Forces

'So we beat on, boats against the current,
borne back ceaselessly into the past'
– F. Scott Fitzgerald, The Great Gatsby

So far, we have met five people all of whom are in search of opportunity. Graham wants new and better clients. Maria is facing a crisis in her career. Karl is struggling to maintain a prosperous livelihood in a changing economy. Janique is a prisoner of time, searching for a way out of the 'Nouveaux Pauvres' trap. Adam is looking for a job.

These five individuals are all being challenged on *courage* as much as they are on *skill*. All five probably have most of the skills they will ever need. There may be some 'asking' skills they need to learn, but these are minimal. However, the *courage* to apply these skills is entirely another matter.

Some readers may rebel at this emphasis on courage. During the writing of this book, we had an interesting email from a lady whose opening line was that she could not understand why people have difficulty asking. Yet in the same email, she goes on to describe a particularly extreme example of the damage caused when someone will not make a request, taken from a *Sunday Times* News Review:

> A lorry driver caused more than £234,000 damages after following his sat nav (GPS) directions down a tiny street in a town's historic Dutch Quarter. The driver was delivering olive oil to a Waitrose supermarket in Colchester, Essex. He ignored traffic signs, jackknifed his lorry on a tight corner and became stuck between Grade 1 listed buildings.

> The bill for his error comprised £200,000 of lost cargo, £25,000 damages to a seventeenth-century house and £20,000 for the lorry trailer, which was written off. The driver from Hungary was given 6 penalty points and fined £40 at Colchester magistrate's court.

Would it not have been better to look at where he was going and stop to ask for a better way to get there? What prevented him from doing this? Was it a language barrier, blind faith in technology, a fear of asking, or something else? Asking costs nothing. Not asking can be expensive!

In their own way, all of our five friends are paying the price of not asking. Jobseekers feel a sense of failure and frustration. Business owners lose money and worry about the future. Independent professionals stumble from feast to famine: periods of overwhelming busyness, alternating with periods of insecurity. As one interim manager dejectedly described it: 'I don't so much have fifteen years' experience, as three years' experience five times over'.

So where is the problem? What stopped the lorry driver from asking? What keeps both Graham and Adam stuck in 'broadcast mode'?

Forces of influence: education

Whether we are aware of it or not, most of us are influenced by our professional education, our upbringing and our culture. For quite a few decades (at least since the end of the Second World War), that culture has prioritised the development of *skill* over the development of *courage*.

In the eyes of most of our parents, education has been the passport to a good job, to prosperity. In recent decades, 'lifelong learning' has been a universal credo, and many pursue skill development well into retirement. Take one look at the diversity of ages in a university class today, and compare that with a class in the 1970s. Since that time, society may well have departed from the altars of other belief systems, but even if traditional churches today stand empty, the worship of knowledge (and skill) in the temples of learning have attracted more followers than ever.

Our thought processes have been shaped in an expertise economy, in a moving stream whose tributaries include family background, culture, expectations and a host of other factors. Many of these thought processes are about *minimising risk*, as opposed to mastery of fear or trying something new. It takes particular courage to swim across this current, and to do things (like asking) that sometimes carry an element of risk. Or at least an element that cannot be controlled.

We can see that there are several currents against which our five friends are swimming, which are carrying them downstream just as they carried the lorry driver into the historic old town of Colchester. It takes a conscious effort of awareness to see these cultural currents, and on top of that we have a range of personality characteristics that colour our lenses: more about that in the next chapter.

Upbringing

When it comes to developing the courage to ask, it's important to appreciate the *strength* of the current that is often flowing against us. Ever since we were children, growing up in the expertise economy, most of us have been learning to **not** ask, often in very subtle ways.

Let's start with Adam. He has spent most of his life sitting in classrooms. Since the age of five, he has been meeting the requirements of the education system: through primary, secondary and tertiary level. Most of these requirements centre around *answering* questions, not asking them. Mathematics is about solving problems. History is learning about the past, and discussing the questions posed. Language study is the knowledge of grammar, the fluent use of correct speech. Computer studies constitute another set of languages and constructs. To learn all of these, you *answer* questions more than you *ask* them.

So, if we work through Adam's timetable over the past sixteen years, how much has he been educated to *ask* questions, and make requests? Leaving aside the Platonic ideals of educators, and the accompanying theories of what education is all about, in how many hours of each week was the student Adam encouraged to pose questions? Does the system encourage *making* requests?

We know the answer. Let's move on. Adam's influence did not stop at the school gates. When Adam goes for a job, who is asking the questions? Who is interviewing whom? How has Adam been taught to get a job interview in the first place?

In his home in Milton Keynes, have his parents encouraged the young Adam to pose challenging questions and make courageous requests? Children are naturally curious, so what happens between the incessant questioning of a three year old and the sullen withdrawal of adolescence?

When we start to think about it, there are a lot of forces that quietly, yet effectively, limit our natural curiosity. As children, we ask quite naturally for what we want; yet as we grow up, we seem to learn that this is somehow 'not OK'.

The cultural current

So if all of that is true in the fairly non-hierarchical, middle class, Anglo-Saxon culture of Milton Keynes, imagine what Janique has been learning?

Janique's educational system in France has been considerably tougher and more challenging than Adam's. The way children are taught is very much 'sit and listen', and you are examined individually every step of the way. Mistakes are pounced on and not encouraged. There is much less sport, drama or teamwork than in Adam's educational experience.

The primary objective of education in France is developing *competence*, not confidence. If the student does well, and gets their qualifications, then perhaps they are 'allowed' to be confident. In psychological terms, this is the confidence that comes from external validation, not internal volition or belief.

In France (as in many parts of the world), this is accompanied by a strict hierarchy, often based on academic achievement. If you have not qualified from a top business school in Paris, you will never occupy a senior management position in many organisations – no matter how much you achieve along the way. Social status and economic status are quite distinct, and the former is usually more highly regarded.

In this context, hierarchy is important: there are some people that Janique will not be allowed to approach, never mind ask for anything. Many foreigners don't notice these distinctions; perhaps they are fortunate to be so excused. Just as they will be forgiven for mixing up the *vous* and the *tu*, their breach of etiquette will be indulged with a polite smile. But Janique will get no such indulgence.

She will be expected to conform to the full rigour of politeness, which does *not* include calling up strangers and asking questions of them. Furthermore, Janique is a failure, and she knows it. The loss of middle-class status is not just an economic failure; it's a social disaster on a monumental scale that few Anglo-Saxon readers can appreciate.

Unwritten rules: habit

Karl is considerably more fortunate. He still has a good job, and he lives in an individualist country where he can approach anyone he wants. If there is a country in Europe where direct requests are easiest and most accepted, it's probably the Netherlands.

Yet Karl is not asking. He too is carrying a heavy cultural burden of responsibility. In his own way, he has inherited thinking patterns that hold him back. For example, he believes he has to begin his meetings with a solution or 'offer' (complete with benefits and evidence) as opposed to going out to market with an enquiry. Why?

Karl has a low tolerance of uncertainty. Once he is outside his comfort zone of programme management, he seeks to impose certainty. He behaves as if he were still inside it. He has not realised that, in order to cultivate opportunity, a different style of dialogue might be required. A more open-ended conversation, where he might be constructing solutions *with* his clients, rather than *for* them.

Like many experienced professionals, Karl has developed habits over the course of his working life: habits about how meetings should happen, habits of planning, habits of structure and habits of dialogue. Many of these habits serve Karl well. But some of these habits are also limiting his search for opportunity. For example, his prospects may be starting to perceive him as 'solution selling' more than they perceive him as being relevant to their agenda.

Maria is also caught up in a struggle with uncertainty. In her case, however, the uncertainty is driven more from within than from the marketplace. How can Maria make requests when she does not yet know what they are? How can she decide whom to ask when she is still clarifying the questions for herself?

Maria feels both confused and conflicted. Furthermore, this confusion is unfamiliar territory to her; she is more accustomed to specific goal setting and achievement. She may even be wondering if this is the early onset of some awful depression, or fatigue-related malaise. She certainly misses the excitement that she used to feel when tackling the next hurdle of the corporate steeplechase.

Graham is depressed. Nursing his hangover, he is obviously low on all types of energy: physical, mental and emotional. Despite his tendency to blame the clients, the Law Society and his ex-wife, he is however not unaware that he has a part to play in his own misfortune. He too is in search of opportunity.

He would probably find opportunities faster if he were to come out of his office, and not try to solve his problem alone. However, as an introvert, he is unlikely to do this. He's more likely to come up with ideas than to 'sell' them. At the very least, he's going to need some support with this. Where can he get that support? He could start by talking to Hannah, who clearly is still loyal and concerned. As we will see later, the cultivation of opportunity is primarily a team sport.

Furthermore, it involves letting go of controlled agendas, having open-ended exploratory conversations, and making requests. Graham is unlikely to sharpen these skills sitting alone in his office, or drinking in his solitary flat. No matter how intelligent he is, opportunity is usually spotted by shifting perspective to that of other people. Graham needs to find a 'Gateway' (or better still, multiple 'Gateways') that will help him create these situations.

As with Maria, this requires a certain amount of letting go of control. Here, once again, our professional upbringing is mainly an individual cultivation of competence, rather than a collective formation of trust. Letting go has not been an integral part of our education. There is very little in our educational process that enhances trust-building. On the contrary, there is a lot that encourages fierce independence, minimising risk, investing maximum effort on oneself and minimising dependence on others or on factors beyond one's control.

Your own stocktake

In summary, our culture, family upbringing and education all come together to create a strong current that carries us away from asking. In some countries, gender is also a factor: that is, men do the asking, while women wait to be asked. Not surprisingly, this manifests itself in pay gaps, representation in top management, and just about anywhere else where the cultivation of opportunity is important.

What messages have you internalised about asking? See the 'thought patterns' listed at the end of this chapter. What other messages have you internalised? Do you identify particularly with Karl, Janique, Adam, Maria or Graham? Are there other issues that represent a strong current for you, that keep you from asking?

Powerful questions have the effect of opening up new channels of thinking and removing blocks to progress. They can help generate self-awareness, a sense of responsibility and facilitate change. Good empathic questioning builds relationships, trust and rapport and in client situations it can clarify, open up new areas of discussion, demonstrate critical understanding of issues and close sales – as long as you can start to unlock the courage to use such a powerful tool.

It's worthwhile being searching and fearless with this stocktake. It's easy to miss our own assumptions about asking questions. If we underestimate the strength of the current, we are unlikely to swim across it. This is often what happens when talented professionals are promoted into opportunity creation roles, and as a result they have a discouraging (rather than encouraging) experience. We have seen this with Karl, and many professionals often suffer the same fate.

Whatever the issues turn out to be, we have to be aware that the current exists. In that way, we won't be too surprised if initially we feel it pushing against us. If Adam is going to try something else, some of his peers may give him quizzical looks. If Graham is going to raise awareness of his firm's services, he is going to have to come out of his shell. If Janique is willing to be creative, she may have to stop doggedly sending CVs and get some rest first. It takes energy to swim across the current.

Unlearning

For Graham or Karl to open new doors, they first have some *unlearning* to do. This takes courage. Both of them see opportunity as resulting from some presentation of themselves and their services. Adam too is searching for an organisation that will find his expertise attractive.

Unlearning is harder than learning. Intelligent people are used to learning: it's always been part of their journey into professional life. But unlearning is more difficult, and takes courage. For example, if Karl has developed the habit of talking people through his presentation or CV, it will feel really uncomfortable to stop doing so. It will be much more tempting to explain why it's necessary to do it.

Maria also has some unlearning to do. She is accustomed to making specific requests, but it's much harder to engage support when you don't know what the problem is. A vague sense that 'something is wrong' does not seem like a sufficient conversation to have – except perhaps with a psychologist – and Maria is a long way away from asking for that kind of help.

What about Janique? She has already abandoned her entire middle-class life; what more does she have to learn or unlearn? In any case, we must remember that with two young children, she does not have much time for anything else. As we will see later, the risk for Janique is that she becomes a prisoner of this story. When endless chores are combined with a sense of having tried everything, a mood of martyrdom and self-pity can set in. No matter how 'justified', this mood needs to be unlearned, just as much as Adam's CV-sending habits.

How do we know what we need to unlearn? The clue usually lies in what is not working, what is no longer serving us. Adam's strategy of sending CVs is clearly not working; indeed it's deepening his frustration and sense of failure. Maria's attempts to understand what's wrong with her current job are not working, she is going around in circles. Graham's list of opportunity tactics on the whiteboard is not working; that's why he is chewing his pencil and worrying about the future. Karl's confidence is being undermined by a growth strategy that is not working.

It takes courage to face up to what is not working for us any more. It takes courage to close a door, even when we know it no longer leads anywhere. Whether it is success (Maria) or failure (Karl), it's not an easy admission to make. Either way, it's a courageous day when we make the declaration. It's always easier to postpone the decision, to look for more evidence or to try something else. Whether in personal life or professional life, it takes real courage to say, 'This is not working. I need to let go of this.'

In those moments, sophisticated procrastination can easily postpone the declaration. Perhaps we feel we didn't try hard enough. Or we cannot face someone else's disappointment or criticism – not to mention our own. Or we dread facing what we see as the inevitable consequences of declaring 'this is not working'.

What might our five friends say, if asked 'what is not working?'

Adam:

'My job-search is not working. It's not getting results and it's damaging my confidence.'

Janique:

'I'm exhausted. I don't have the energy to find anything better. And I feel I am failing my children.'

Karl:

'I'm frustrated. I've tried everything and I'm worried about what will happen now.'

Maria:

'I don't know how to answer... I think I've lost my way.'

Graham:

'I'm bored and depressed. I should be doing something to create opportunity. And I can't.'

So before we start the second leg of our journey, what declaration(s) would you like to make about your present state? What is not working for you? The essential declarations usually take some courage. It takes even more courage to write them down.

Whenever you try something different, the first thing you experience is **resistance and discomfort**. This may come from others, or from yourself. If Adam goes for a run, his first experience will be tired muscles. A sense of failure may overwhelm Janique the moment she stops sending CVs. Graham may find it difficult to sit down with Hannah and face the truth of their situation. Karl may feel exposed when he starts a meeting with a question rather than a presentation.

Can *you* live with discomfort? What is it that makes this discomfort worthwhile? Who can you rely on, during the initial phase of discomfort and resistance?

If you can live with some discomfort, the muscles of courage are already starting to develop.

Thought patterns about asking

The psychology of asking – what does it mean to ask a question? Possible thought patterns about *asking:*

- *People should know what I want – I shouldn't have to ask*
- *Only children ask lots of questions*
- *If I ask a question it means I am stalling and don't have an answer*
- *I'm embarrassed that I don't know the answer to this question*
- *I am stupid because I don't know the answer to this question*
- *Am I asking the right question?*
- *What if everyone else knows the answer?*
- *I am interested*
- *I am keen to understand the issues further*
- *I want to check my understanding*
- *It's expected*
- *It's polite*
- *It's a reflex*
- *It's rude*
- *It will put people on the spot and make them uncomfortable*
- *I might have to justify why I've asked*
- *I'm not being empathic if I have to ask how someone feels or sees the situation*
- *I'm not listening*

Others? Which thought patterns will serve you best?

Part two

9

Seven Gateways to Courage

'Life shrinks or expands in proportion to one's courage'
– Anaïs Nin

If you have been following the story so far, by now you will have a strong sense of just how big the 'courage challenge' is. Most people are unlikely to start making courageous requests overnight, and even if they do, they can expect some push-back from colleagues, peers and clients.

Indeed it is a paradox of change that once you have come to the monumental decision to change something about yourself, others will often try to stop you from changing. People like consistency and they want you to stay the way you are – predictability equals safety. So to be prepared for change, you must be prepared for push-back. Facing this push-back and resistance from others requires courage. We are therefore going to concentrate on courage for a while; we will come back to 'asking' later.

Courage is the principal root from which opportunity and prosperity grow. We defined courage in Chapter 1 as strength in the face of risk, pain or grief. Without courage, the asking never happens. Everybody has courage. However, our ability to *access* courage depends on a web of factors such as personality characteristics, values, beliefs and social forces. These enable us to access certain 'gateways' to courage more easily than others. This is what we are now going to explore.

Over the next few chapters, we are going to present seven 'gateways' to courage for consideration, in much the same way as we might consider how to access a walled castle. We have chosen this castle metaphor with some care. First, courage is not that easy to access, even for those who desire this quality intensely. Wishing for courage does not magically create it: it usually takes more than affirmation to build this strength. When risk appears and the heart beats faster, an affirmation is quickly forgotten. Something more is needed, and the next few chapters will explore this in detail.

Second, the walls of the castle are well defended: by forces such as culture, upbringing and habit. We saw some of these forces in the previous chapter. It might also be worth adding that many aspects of life in Western Europe are more about *diminishing risk* than developing courage. For example, it is more likely that a young professional gets taught to play it safe than to accept the possibility of failure and be encouraged to try, anyway. If a young graduate wants to abandon a 'safe' career in a traditional profession, and instead pursue a career in the arts or another sector seen as 'risky', what advice are they likely to receive?

Third, there is a choice of gateways to the castle (courage), and once you are 'in', it often appears that all other gateways are magically open from the inside. Once you possess a sufficient level of courage, the issue of courage almost disappears and you feel free to do whatever you want. The 'wall' is only a problem from the outside: all the gateways are usually accessible from the inside.

Why should this be the case? Why is courage easier to access once you have done something courageous?

We'd like to suggest that this phenomenon is to do with fear. Fear keeps you in the state of the unknown. If you act despite fear, you take away the unknown. Sometimes you succeed and sometimes you fail but you replace unknown with known. In many situations your brain assesses: is knowing (regardless of how acceptable the outcome is to you personally) better than not knowing? Often the answer is yes, because knowing enables action – you perceive a level of control. Of course this may not be the reality; you may not be in control. Nonetheless, the feeling produced is one of control.

In the following seven chapters, we will outline seven of these gateways to courage. We certainly don't pretend that these are the only ways into the castle, but they account for the majority of routes by which professionals find the necessary strength to do what they need to do. The gateways are:

1. Connection to Others
2. Purpose and Meaning
3. Influence and Communication Skill
4. Self-awareness
5. Self-discipline
6. Curiosity and Creativity
7. Physical Stamina

To be courageous, do we need all of these? Certainly not. Depending on personality characteristics, some of these gateways may be more accessible than others. While all of the gateways are available to everyone, each person usually finds some gateways easier to get through than others.

Nevertheless, we will illustrate why it's useful to access courage via *several* gateways, rather than relying on a single one. For example, some people rely heavily on the first gateway: Connection to Others. They thrive when surrounded by competent, caring adults, and as long as they are so surrounded, they may not feel the need to explore the other gateways.

However, should they experience the sudden loss of key people –whether through death, divorce or redundancy – their courage can be seriously impacted. At the very moment when courage is most needed, their access (via the gateway of Connection to Others) appears blocked. However, if they can access courage via other gateways (for example, Purpose, Self-discipline or Physical Stamina), this can provide the strength to see them through a difficult time.

That said, each person usually finds some gateways more accessible than others. The example above (that is, getting courage from a sense of connection) is often the case with extroverts, who get their energy and encouragement from being around others. By contrast, introverts may *need* courage to be around others (remember the definition of courage – it may be 'painful' to have company foisted on you as an introvert), so this gateway may not be equally accessible to them.

However, just because a gateway is most *accessible* does not mean that it is most *beneficial.* The introvert we have just referred to may derive tremendous benefit from being around others, just as a playful extrovert may derive courage from a moderate amount of gentle self-discipline. This is another reason why we recommend that you explore all gateways: even those that are less accessible. You may get surprising benefit from surprising places.

Personality characteristics: a short introduction

In describing personality characteristics, we are going to stick with the basic 'Big Five' most widely used and accepted by psychologists in recent years. The Costa and McCrae five-factor model has the soundest empirical grounding and while not without controversy, is the least controversial model. The five-factor model also links to MBTI[2], a tool many readers will be familiar with. However, the Big Five model provides a more commonly shared conceptual framework with more empirical evidence than MBTI and this is why we have used it.

While there is a significant body of literature supporting this five-factor model of personality, researchers don't always agree on the exact labels for each dimension. It is important to note that each of the five personality factors represents a range between two extremes. For example, extroversion represents a continuum between extreme extroversion and extreme introversion. In the real world, most people lie somewhere in between the two polar ends of each dimension. People *tend* towards a certain end of the scale but are perfectly capable of displaying seemingly opposite characteristics within themselves. This is perfectly normal.

People are a mass of contradictions. If we accept this, it becomes much easier to see where our tendencies lie. In life we seek to be absolute – consistency is a prized and valued quality. The acceptance that we are made up of a whole series of contradictions can be a great 'loosener of chains'. If I accept I *tend* to behave as an extrovert – it allows me my cherished and very real moments

---

2. Four of the MBTI scales are related to the Big Five personality traits. These correlations show that E-I and S-N are strongly related to extroversion and openness respectively, while T-F and J-P are moderately related to agreeableness and conscientiousness respectively. The emotional stability dimension of the Big Five is largely absent from the original MBTI.

of introversion while still being me. If I say I have to be one or the other – this grates and I seek to object to everything about being an extrovert because my piece of contradictory introvert has nowhere to go – de facto I can't possibly be an extrovert.

Contradictions and exceptions make us colourful and who we are. In thinking of the gateways that may be easiest to access, think about your tendency but also be prepared to use the colourfulness of contradiction to great effect. Situation also plays its part. Behaviour involves an interaction between a person's underlying personality and situational variables. The situation that a person finds himself or herself in plays a major role in how the person reacts, so personality may not account for how you entirely access courage – your situation may influence this too.

A note of caution is required in reading these definitions. The language used by psychologists and personality experts can seem to imply judgement because of the way certain words have been accepted or colloquialised into our everyday language. There should be no judgement intended but the definitions need reading with some care, remembering there is not a right or wrong end of the scale. Personality is a sum total composite of characteristics, not a single characteristic. It's often the interplay of characteristics that makes a person who they are.

However, it is an inescapable truth that some aspects of society do favour certain characteristics – for example, extroversion over introversion. Our desire to 'fit in' could overwhelm an accurate assessment of our own personality characteristics and hamper understanding of those gateways that may be easiest to access. If you find yourself reacting to any of the words in the next few paragraphs, you may wish to explore this further.

'OCEAN' is a useful acronym to help remember the Big Five dimensions. Let's look at each of the scales in turn:

O – Openness to experience: 'Curious' vs 'Consistent'
C – Conscientiousness: 'Efficient and Organised' vs 'Easy-going and Spontaneous'
E – Extroversion: 'Outgoing' vs 'Solitary'
A – Agreeableness: 'Adaptable' vs 'Challenging'
N – Neuroticism: 'Sensitive' vs 'Assured'

Openness to experience: This is the extent to which you tend towards being **curious** vs a tendency towards being **consistent**.

People high on openness tend to be more abstract and have a general appreciation for art, emotion, adventure, unusual ideas, imagination, curiosity and variety of experience. They find change easy to accept. Often intellectually curious, they tend to be imaginative, creative and value emotional experience. People with low scores on openness tend to have more conventional, traditional interests. They prefer the straightforward over the complex or ambiguous and often describe themselves as rational. A tendency away from openness indicates people who prefer familiarity over novelty; they are conservative and more resistant to change and they tend to be more practical and attentive to detail.

Conscientiousness: This is the extent to which you tend towards being **efficient and organised** vs the tendency to be **easy-going and spontaneous.**

People tending towards high conscientiousness show self-discipline, act dutifully and aim for achievement against measures or outside expectations. The trait shows a preference for planned rather than spontaneous behaviour. It influences the way in which people control, regulate and direct their impulses. A tendency towards high conscientiousness describes people able to focus attention on sustained, repetitive, goal-focused behaviour. People with lower conscientiousness scores tend to come across as more carefree and less rule-bound. Their minds can flip more easily from track to track.

Procrastination can be a key problem at both ends of this spectrum, but for very different reasons. Those with high conscientiousness tend to experience perfectionism and get stuck by a fear of failure or making a mistake. As leaders, they may find it hard to recognise that the fear of failure is creating a procrastination pattern. At the opposite end of the spectrum, those who are easy-going and spontaneous are less methodical and more casual. Their procrastination is more likely to be driven by distraction rather than fear of failure.

Extroversion: This is the tendency to be **outgoing** and take energy from the company of others vs the tendency to be **solitary** and find the company of others energy zapping.

People with the tendency to seek out stimulation and the company of others usually describe themselves as extroverts. This characteristic displays itself by engagement in the external world. Extroverts enjoy being with people, and are often perceived as full of energy. They tend to be enthusiastic, action-oriented individuals, and not surprisingly are more likely to assert themselves and lead others. Introverts are comfortable without the social exuberance and activity levels of extroverts. They often seem quiet, deliberate and less involved in the social world. This lack of outward social involvement should not however be interpreted as shyness. Introverts need less stimulation than extroverts and more time alone. They can be equally active and energetic, simply not socially. Introverts tend instead towards introspection and insight.

Some people move easily from working alone to working with others. The term 'ambivert' has recently been coined to describe those who flip between 'extrovert' and 'introvert' behaviours. With extroverts, they may appear introverted (even overwhelmed) when surrounded by more extreme extroverts; while with introverts they may well appear more outgoing when surrounded by extreme introverts.

Agreeableness: This is the tendency to be **adaptable** and cooperative vs **challenging** and mindful of self-interest.

People's agreeableness reflects their general concern for social harmony. Agreeable people value getting along with others. They are generally considerate of others' feelings or positions, friendly, generous, helpful, and willing to compromise their interests with others. Agreeable people also have an optimistic view of human nature and can be sometimes called naive. Individuals whose tendency is towards the opposite end of the scale tend to place self-interest above getting along with others. They are generally less concerned with others' well-being or feelings, and are less likely to extend themselves for other people. Sometimes their scepticism about others' motives causes them to be suspicious and uncooperative. Their strengths lie in traditional forms of negotiation where single-mindedness and self-belief are required, over and above harmony. They relate to authority with scepticism and are tough and guarded. They are usually persistent, competitive, need to win and to be seen to win.

Neuroticism: This is the tendency towards being **sensitive** vs being **assured** and emotionally stable.

Your neuroticism score estimates the point at which your fight or flight response is triggered. Those with higher scores have a shorter trigger and can take less stress before, for example, displaying anger. People who tend towards neuroticism are more emotionally reactive. They are more likely to interpret situations as threatening, and minor frustrations as difficult. They tend to experience more negative emotional reactions (but it has been argued more positive ones too). They come across as less emotionally controlled in decision making and worry more than those tending towards the 'assured' end of the scale.

Individuals who score low in neuroticism have a longer fuse and are able to absorb more stress before it shows. They are less easily upset and are less emotionally reactive and more thick-skinned and impulse-controlled. When they do get upset, they recover more quickly. They tend to be calm, emotionally stable, and free from persistent negative feelings. However, freedom from negative feelings does not mean that low scorers experience a lot of positive feelings – instead it's believed they have a more bounded emotional range.

People with low neuroticism scores tend to be more resilient and free of stress, displaying a more optimistic outlook. They are less likely to exhibit addictive tendencies, such as food, alcohol, shopping, tobacco, etc., and they are not easily embarrassed.

The Big Five traits are remarkably universal. Studies have shown for example that the five dimensions could be accurately used to describe personality across people from more than fifty different cultures. Based on this research, many psychologists now believe that the five personality dimensions are not only universal, they also have biological origins. Evolutionary explanations suggest that they represent the most important qualities that shape our social landscape. They certainly shape our ability to access courage.

In the following chapters, we will see the Big Five characteristics in action. We will explore each gateway, one by one, and see how these gateways can assist our five friends to develop the courage to ask, so that they can cultivate the opportunities they need.

Before we do, you may wish to review the Big Five scales above, and consider your own tendencies towards each of the dimensions. Remember we are not absolutes and situational factors and sheer inconsistency will impact on how you behave. Understanding your tendencies will give you clues on how to start to access courage, and which of the gateways will be most accessible for you.

Exercise

You might find it useful to profile your own personality against these characteristics:

	HIGH ←	→ MID ←	→LOW
O:	Curious . . . . .Consistent		
C:	Efficient and Organised . . . . .Spontaneous and Easygoing		
E:	Outgoing. . . . . Solitary		
A:	Adaptable . . . . Challenging		
N:	Sensitive . . . . Assured		

It's generally useful to start with those aspects of your personality that are most pronounced. Which of the five characteristics did you instantly identify as part of your make-up? Did Openness jump off the page at you, or is your Neuroticism the key to who you are? This is the place to start. Position yourself on each scale.

Relating gateways to personality characteristics

As already outlined, certain gateways are easier for some than for others. We will go further into this subject in the chapters that follow. For the moment here is a summary – by personality characteristic – of the gateways that are most accessible for each trait.

Some gateways crop up across the spectrum of a single personality characteristic. For example, 'Influence and Communication Skill' is equally useful across the spectrum of 'Openness': to both 'Curious' and to 'Consistent' people.

However, please note that there may be many exceptions to the tables below; they are not absolutes. You are the best judge of yourself and your own situation. Nevertheless, many people find the following guideline useful – particularly those in urgent need of courage.

Characteristic: Openness to Experience

Tendency towards novelty and variety as opposed to familiarity and routine.

Most accessible gateways for CURIOUS people:	Most accessible gateways for CONSISTENT people:
Connection to Others	Purpose and Meaning
Curiosity and Creativity	Self-discipline
Self-awareness	Physical Stamina
(gateway accessible to full spectrum i.e. everybody) Influence and Communication Skill	

Characteristic: Conscientiousness

Preference for achievement in a planned and methodical way, as opposed to spontaneous and unstructured behaviour.

Most accessible gateways for EFFICIENT AND ORGANISED people:	Most accessible gateways for EASY-GOING AND SPONTANEOUS people:
Purpose and Meaning	Connection to Others
Self-awareness	Curiosity and Creativity
Self-discipline	
(gateways accessible to full spectrum i.e. everybody) Influence and Communication Skill Physical Stamina	

Characteristic: Extroversion

Tendency towards wanting to be around other people vs wanting to be alone.

Most accessible gateways for OUTGOING people:	Most accessible gateways for SOLITARY people:
Connection to Others	Purpose and Meaning
Influence and Communication Skill	Self-discipline
Physical Stamina	
(gateways accessible to full spectrum i.e. everybody)	
Self-awareness (finding it in different ways)	
Curiosity and Creativity	

Characteristic: Agreeableness

Tendency towards being cooperative rather than being competitive.

Most accessible gateways for ADAPTABLE people:	Most accessible gateways for CHALLENGING people:
Connection to Others	Purpose and Meaning
Influence and Communication Skill	Self-discipline
Self-awareness	Physical Stamina
(gateways accessible to full spectrum i.e. everybody)	
Curiosity and Creativity	

Characteristic: Neuroticism

Tendency towards volatile emotional states/sensitivity
vs calm and assurance.

Most accessible gateways for SENSITIVE people:	Most accessible gateways for ASSURED people:
Connection to Others	Influence and Communication Skill
Purpose and Meaning	Self-discipline
	Physical Stamina

(gateways accessible to full spectrum i.e. everybody)
Self-awareness (favouring mid-range scores, avoiding extreme poles)
Curiosity and Creativity

Exercise

Now that you have identified your personality characteristics (previous exercise), you may find it useful to circle the gateways that crop up most frequently for you.

Every gateway is open to all, and the more gateways you open, the greater your access to courage. Furthermore, your courage will be more sustainable and you will be able to deal with situations in which a favourite gateway may appear blocked.

As we describe each gateway in detail over the course of the next seven chapters, may we ask you to consider the following questions?

1. FIT: How accessible do I find this gateway? How does this fit with my personality characteristics? In what ways can I already see myself getting courage (and encouragement) this way?
2. USEFULNESS: To what further benefits might this gateway lead me? How might my life/career be expanded further in this way? What requests would I be able to make more easily? What difference could this make?

You may find it useful to see the full matrix, which can be summarised as follows:

	Openness	Conscientiousness	Extroversion	Agreeableness	Neuroticism
1 Connection to Others favours the...	Curious	Easy-going and Spontaneous	Outgoing	Adaptable	Sensitive
2 Purpose and Meaning favours the...	Consistent	Efficient and Organised	Solitary	Challenging	Sensitive
3 Influence and Communication Skill favours the...	(ALL)	(ALL)	Outgoing	Adaptable	Assured
4 Self-awareness favours the...	Curious	Efficient and Organised	(ALL, finding it in different ways)	Adaptable	(ALL favouring mid-scores)
5 Self-discipline favours the...	Consistent	Efficient and Organised	Solitary	Challenging	Assured
6 Curiosity and Creativity favours the...	Curious	Easy-going and Spontaneous	(ALL)	(ALL)	(ALL)
7 Physical Stamina favours the...	Consistent	(ALL)	Outgoing	Challenging	Assured

A final word about gateways: we don't believe these are the *only* access points to courage. No doubt you will discover some of your own. Research is constantly refining the links between personality characteristics and courage. Nevertheless, we have found that in our work supporting professionals to cultivate opportunity, these seven gateways constitute a strong starting point.

We now begin our exploration with the first gateway: Connection to Others.

10
First Gateway – Connection to Others

'We are afraid to care too much; for fear that the other person does not care at all' – Eleanor Roosevelt

Few people dream of success without someone with whom to share the champagne. It's good to know that somewhere out there, there are 'competent and caring adults' who care about us. Even if we don't see them regularly, we derive encouragement from our dialogue with them – even when that dialogue is occasionally in our imagination.

Some people need more connection than others. For many, a dinner-table conversation with good friends (or family members) will be the epicentre of a happy life. Others need less connection and can manage long periods of solitude; yet almost every human being needs to know that someone somewhere cares about them.

Connection to Others is our ability to actively recruit people who can help us or fulfil us in some way. Even the most altruistic of people get fulfilment from connecting with others. The skills required to connect well include: an ability to make and keep relationships; to access positive peer support; and the capacity to take on different roles within different relationships. These skills are underpinned by our attachment patterns (the dynamics of long-term relationships between humans formed in early childhood) and our attitude to trust. Empathy and listening skills – discussed in Chapter 12 (Influence and Communication Skill) are also important building blocks of connection to others.

Many of us draw energy and encouragement from other people. This is why *esprit de corps* and teamwork are so important in the army, in sports, in rehab, anywhere that courage is required. When people are feeling low, they can access the energy of the group… even on those days when their individual resources seem to have abandoned them.

On the other hand, 'enforced' isolation is painful. Particularly for those whose personality characteristics include extroversion or agreeableness, a lack of connection to others can rapidly diminish their capacity for action. The energy that comes from collaboration with other people is missing.

Furthermore, when it comes to a sense of connection with others, *quality* seems to be more important than *quantity*. Three good friends may do more for courage than 300 Facebook friends. When we are secure with our 'champions', when we know that a few well-placed people think well of us, then our capacity to take courageous action is enlarged.

Fortunately for us, we live in an age when we can have *both* quantity and quality. We don't have to choose. It is possible to have a few close friends *and* several hundred friends on social media.

Forces of isolation

Yet we also live in an age where there are many forces of isolation in action, both at home and at work. For example, the number of single-person households has risen dramatically. According to the market research firm Euromonitor International, the number of people living alone globally is skyrocketing, rising from about 153 million in 1996 to 277 million in 2011 – an increase of around 80 per cent in 15 years. In the UK, 34 per cent of households now have one person living in them.

Work friendships are often transient. An international career spanning several countries can leave a fifty-something adult wondering where she or he belongs. Divorce and separation splits friendships as well as families. In many marriages, one partner often looks after the social diary, and the other partner does not realise their isolation until death or divorce strikes. Then they are suddenly left with empty weekends and no holiday plans, enduring their loss on their own.

For young men in particular, many friendships do not survive beyond college and early work life. Many will find that they have fewer real friends at their thirtieth birthday than they had celebrating their twenty-first. With a socially constructed tendency away from relationships and towards a focus on achievement (no, we don't believe it's biologically hard-wired!), it's all too easy for young men to undervalue relatedness as a measure of happiness or success and to lose contact and feel isolated.

Courage plays a significant part in the willingness to keep in contact. With every passing month that Adam spends out of work, it's harder for him to meet up with college friends. Not just because of lack of confidence; travel costs and escalating tastes for eating out can also drive a practical wedge into many a friendship. It takes particular courage to stay in touch with friends who seem to be doing better than oneself.

Each of our five friends will have to contend with differing forces of isolation. This should not be confused with physical isolation. Research shows that it's the quality, not the quantity of social interactions that most defines isolation. What matters is not whether we *are* physically alone, but whether we *feel* alone. Indeed, it's often those in larger cities and larger companies who feel isolation most. The more people around you, the easier it is to feel lonely in a crowd.

People perceived as 'successful' are not immune to feelings of isolation. It can be genuinely 'lonely at the top'. As a global director, Maria may well feel that people only respect her because of the role that she occupies. Without that role, would they still want to see her? Would they listen to what she has to say? We often imagine that business leaders (or good-looking people, or those with money) are fortunate to never be isolated for long. In many cases, the opposite is true. Even when surrounded with admirers, 'successful' people often feel that the admiration is not really for 'them' but for the role they occupy, or the image that they project.

So when people feel isolated, what happens to their courage? How does isolation affect their ability to withstand difficult change or setbacks?

As we will see elsewhere, whenever a gateway is closed, a person becomes more reliant on the other gateways. So, successful people who feel isolated may become reliant on their past achievements and/ or their next vision of success. In doing so, they may of course become even more isolated. They may withdraw into former (or future) glory, and in doing so may not be very effective in the present.

They may seek other escape routes. Perhaps they will do another training course, which will at least give them some mental stimulation. Or they will start dreaming about the future. Perhaps this explains why lottery tickets boom in recession; in the US, sales of lottery tickets increased by $1billion in 2010 alone.

Whether isolated by success or by failure, the loss of connection to others invariably diminishes courage. When isolated, a person is less able to access the external forces sometimes required to kick-start self-belief and enable 'self-determined action'. If I feel discouraged, I may think 'what's the point?', therefore I do less and become more isolated, therefore I feel more discouraged and so on...This has a knock-on effect on a sense of meaning and purpose (for example, 'What's the use?') and this diminishes courage even further. The negative spiral described above can easily result in creating depression, fatigue and low physical energy.

People who are unemployed are particularly vulnerable. Workplaces provide access to other human beings and opportunities to collaborate with them. Even if many of these interactions are transactional, there is at least the possibility of making a human connection with the occasional client or colleague. We may perhaps recognise a face on our regular commute to work, or greet the assistant in the newsagent's. At the very least, the employed (like Janique) are leaving their house or apartment. For the unemployed, however, it is all too easy to stay at home, as indeed Adam is finding.

However, employment does not always result in a sense of connection. Many workplaces are transactional in nature. If you work in a call-centre, at a helpdesk or in an accounts function, what are the chances of forming a personal relationship with your client? If you are in a back office secretarial function like Janique, to what extent will you have interaction at all? Even if he wants to, how often will Graham be able to have a human connection with his clients?

Needless to say, many turn to online social media… if they are allowed to do so during working hours, of course. This is not the book in which to enter that debate. Social media can play a very important role in connecting people, and particularly in enabling people to stay in touch. But they can also emphasise one's isolation. If you are getting no feedback on your blog, or your status updates go unnoticed, what does that do for your sense of connection? No matter how savvy we are, online media can be a double-edged sword.

So how is your sense of connection? As we work through each of the seven gateways, may we ask you to rate this gateway for you as follows:

4 =   *Excellent, a real and consistent source of encouragement*
3 =   *Good, usually positive, perhaps intermittently so, maybe not always surrounded by ideal people*
2 =   *Fair, experiencing periods of isolation, or people who drain energy/discourage*
1 or 0 =   *Low, I need to get my encouragement from elsewhere*

As you do your scoring, please exclude dependants such as children. The encouragement they give will appear under Purpose and Meaning later on. This gateway is about the encouragement you get from a sense of connection with competent and caring *adults*, who also care about you.

Likewise, your score will be diminished by negative people or 'crazy makers' in your life. If you are the person who has to *provide* all the encouragement, listening and support, this reduces your score.

While you are deciding, let's hear what our five friends from Part One might say:

Adam:
'No, I don't identify with those young men above. I'm lucky to have good friends, with whom I can be myself. And I get on well with my parents: even if Mum nags from time to time and Dad can be a bit aloof. If I got a job tomorrow, they are the first people I would call with the news.

'Yes, I do notice a few people dropping off at the fringes, usually because they have moved away or got busy with a new job. So all in all; I would score this with a 3.'

Janique:

'This is a painful start for me. It's probably my fault, but my first reaction was a zero. The destruction of the past few years has been total. My boss is OK, but there is a polite distance there, and to be honest that suits me just now.

'Thinking about my children, I was going to change it to a 1. But then I stopped when you said that this referred to adults only. I guess there are some friends with whom I could get back in touch, though I don't want to just now. But they are there. So I will leave it at a 1.'

Karl:

'No problems here. Good family and friends. Even with the current difficulties, good connection with work colleagues. There is nothing here that stops me making requests. So it's a 4.'

Graham:

'I go with the flow. No, I don't feel a huge sense of connection with other people. And I don't particularly look to others for opportunity, either; I believe in availing of opportunity when it comes. This translates into how I think about my business. Things happen when they happen; it's impossible to predict when.

'So I am scoring this as a 1. Obviously, my life is not devoid of connection, yet I would admit there is room for a lot more. But who can you trust?'

Maria:

'I would not regard myself as isolated. Yet I do acknowledge that I tend to share only my "processed thoughts" with people, not the raw "unprocessed" fragments. If I consider my sense of connection in these terms, perhaps it's not so good. I also tend to compartmentalise; so I talk to my husband about home-stuff, my friends about life-stuff and my colleagues about work-stuff.

'So who knows the real me? Perhaps a 2?'

Trust

As Maria and Graham are discovering in different ways, there is a big piece of this around trust, about which entire books have been written. In order to have a sense of connection with people, we have to be able to trust them enough. If Maria is so carefully managing her relationships, both at work and at home, to what extent is she really connecting with people?

With those who really care, we don't have to 'edit'. We can report life as we find it, and change our interpretation next week. We don't feel that we will be judged, excluded or diminished in their eyes. With them, we feel safe even in uncertainty and in doubt. We can speak in contradictions; what we say does not always have to make sense. We know that, apart from calamity, they will be there for us – just as we will be there for them.

Of course, such people are few and far between. If we have between three and five of these people in our lives, we can genuinely count ourselves lucky. Our status with them is not contingent on success or failure. With real friends, do we care how much money they are making, or whether they succeed and get that next promotion? Is it not reasonable that they also think equally well of us?

On the flip side, we have to be prepared to be there for them, too. If we expect others to not judge us too harshly, then the likelihood is that we will also be required to be equally generous with them. To what extent has Graham been available for others? How might this be relevant to his current situation?

For all these reasons, a strong sense of connection with others can be a gateway to courage. When times are tough, we can call these people and draw strength from them. If we are about to embark on an uncertain course of action (such as asking questions and making requests), we can get genuine support and encouragement from these people... even if they don't have the skills or contacts to help us specifically.

To kick-start self-esteem, we need someone to believe in us first. This is the paradox of self-esteem: it seems we learn to esteem ourselves by borrowing validation from significant 'others': a parent, a friend, a teacher, a coach, a colleague. Even for those who are confident, it helps when others believe in us.

No matter how confident a professional may seem to be, those who are extremely self-reliant may sometimes be operating out of fear. Graham may well be drawing his courage and self-image from his former achievements, or his expertise; and hence his confidence may well be contingent on the validation of other people. He may fear disagreement with others.

In the French language, the same word '*confiance*' is used both for trust and for confidence. Something for Janique to reflect on. If she could find a way to break her current isolation, might that open some of those 'hidden doors' for which she is searching? Even if these are not doors to immediate opportunity, perhaps some genuine trust and sharing would restore her confidence and create new ideas. Perhaps even bringing a sense of fun and play into her life, this in turn often inspires new energy and creativity.

With this particular gateway, connecting and feeling a sense of connection relies in part on how the 'other' you are connecting to feels towards you. Your extroversion score and openness score are most important here. You will find it easier to connect to those with similar tendencies on Extroversion and Openness – you will sense who these people are, so therefore we suggest you don't force connections that appear hard work; in any case, you are unlikely to succeed.

Connection to Others is a particularly important gateway for those with the following personality characteristics:

1. Openness dimension: Curious (vs Consistent): Interaction with others enhances their openness to experience: creating learning, variety and new perspective. Courage builds as new possibilities open up, and professionals find new applications for their skills. Of our five friends, who would you say is most curious?

In very different ways, Maria and Graham are both open to experience. Both possess high degrees of curiosity. Maria has risen to senior management in corporate life, which entails not only intellectual talent, but also ability for abstraction and a tolerance for ambiguity. Graham is more introverted (and right now he's depressed) yet he is intellectually curious by nature and enjoys new experiences. Adam, Janique and Karl all tend more towards being 'Consistent' in their habits.

2. Conscientiousness dimension: Easy-going and Spontaneous (vs Efficient and Organised): People with this characteristic are often popular, and therefore find connection to others easy and accessible. However, they are not always aware of this popularity, particularly if they tend towards 'Sensitive' rather than 'Assured' on the 'Neuroticism' scale. One of our friends fits this description: who is it?

Graham is by far the most easy-going of the five, yet does not perceive how popular he is (or could be). He is certainly not 'conscientious': if it were not for Hannah, he would be lost. All of the others are quite organised and efficient in their own way.

3. Extroversion dimension: Outgoing (vs Solitary): This is an obvious gateway for extroverts, and they usually find it quite naturally. Several of our friends are likely to do so; who are they?

Karl and Maria are clearly outgoing people. Janique may be also; we simply don't know yet. Outgoing people find it easy to meet others, and derive energy and encouragement from doing so. Connection to others is a powerful source of energy and encouragement for outgoing extroverts.

4. Agreeableness dimension: Adaptable (vs Challenging): Again, an obvious gateway for adaptable people who prioritise social harmony, and one from which they usually benefit enormously. Of our five friends, who might this be? This scale is about the degree to which one is drawn by concern for others.

Adam, Janique and Maria would all score high on Agreeableness, and hence would be described as friendly and 'Adaptable'. Whether they have friends or not, they are close to their family members and care about them. Janique is close to her children, Adam still has good relationships with his parents and Maria, despite her busy life, still has friends, too.

5. Neuroticism dimension: Sensitive (vs Assured): These people often derive stability and encouragement from having a few people believe in them. Of the five, who are you thinking of?

Janique and Graham are probably the least self-assured of our five friends, and so would both be described as 'Sensitive'. Both can therefore access courage via 'Connection to Others', through the belief that others have in them. As long as they are willing to make that connection, of course: right now, neither Janique nor Graham are doing so.

In summary, while all of our friends will get benefit via the Connection to Others gateway, Graham, Janique and Maria will find it particularly useful: Graham to stabilise his mood swings, Janique with her isolation and Maria to get some new perspective.

Exercise

Based on your personality characteristics, score this gateway in terms of how accessible you decide it is for you. Is it High, Medium or Low?

Top tips to help you develop Connection to Others

1. Making time to connect with others It's a task like any other. Set appropriate goals (not necessarily quantitative ones, but numbers will probably feature) and monitor them. This is especially important if you find connecting hard. For example you may decide to follow up five old contacts each day for a two-week period. Or you may decide to find a colleague or a friend to mentor or coach you. Assess your progress against your goals – are you accessing courage through your connectedness to others? Note that connecting and staying connected are two separate things.

2. Balancing quantity and quality There is no question that connecting to others helps cultivate opportunity: we often hear of opportunities via other people. But careful balance is needed between quality and quantity. Too many and you are not truly connecting (other than clicking a LinkedIn button, for example); too few and you are not reaching a diverse and large enough set of contacts from which to cultivate opportunities. There is no magic number of contacts. Connecting with others can be intrinsically motivating for extroverts and a necessary 'forced' activity for introverts. Your contact volumes and their quality will naturally reflect your personality – learn to offset this to best effect, in ways that work for you.

3. Being authentic and genuine When we talk about connection to others we aren't talking about superficial 'networking'. We are talking about seeking a genuine connection to other people that fulfils you in some way. This entails being honest about what you stand for rather than being socially polite. It involves a clear sense of who you are and how you operate in your marketplace. It's not possible to be all things to all people.

4. Developing your ability to trust and be trustworthy Starting with point 3 is a good basis for trust building. Being prepared to 'give something away' about yourself also helps. Another approach is to allow yourself to 'loosen the reins' and let go of trying to control situations; for example, by asking exploratory questions and seeing what happens. Positive self-talk can help you see the opportunities that arise when people don't do things the same way you would. Trust develops when you do what you say you will do (reliability), and also when you apologise when you are wrong.

11
Second Gateway – Purpose and Meaning

'Efforts and courage are not enough without purpose and
direction' – John F. Kennedy

There is an old story about three medieval stonemasons. The first is asked what he is doing. 'I'm cutting stone,' he answers. The second is asked what he is doing. 'I'm building a wall,' he says. The third is asked what he is doing. 'I'm building a cathedral,' he replies.

Of the three, which stonemason is most likely to go to work on a rainy Monday morning with the greatest courage and vigour? All other things being equal (and as we will see, there are quite a few 'other things'), we can safely assume that the sense of purpose that inspires the third mason will be significant indeed.

Many medieval stonemasons never lived to see the finished results of their work. It took entire generations of architects and craftsmen to build cathedrals and palaces. Yet their sense of meaning and purpose allowed them to conceive projects that would be rarely conceived today.

However, *purpose* and *meaning* are not one and the same. To have **meaning** is to search for validation and a sense of belonging in a larger reality, or the opportunity to learn more about the world. **Purpose** is the pursuit of efficacy, competence, freedom (yours), constraint (others) or dominance.

A purpose can be a simple objective, such as to get a job or achieve a result. Meaning is more about significance: the way in which your purpose has worth, importance or value for you. The days of a busy manager may be filled with purpose, but that does not necessarily imply that his or her days have meaning. Furthermore, not everyone seeks meaning in work – even those who would claim that a sense of purpose is important to them.

Whatever about the differences, however, both *purpose* and *meaning* are similar in one important respect: they answer the question, 'Why are you doing what you do?' Whether the stone-mason saw the cathedral in terms of purpose, or of meaning, he was certainly conscious of the end-result of his labour. He was motivated by a vision of what he was building.

When we see the 'why' of doing something, we can often deal with the most tedious of tasks. If we want to buy that house badly enough, we go through hoops of paperwork and administration to satisfy the requirements of lenders and lawyers. If someone really wants that promotion, they will work for it. In the pursuit of a 'wow design', a passionate designer may well forget to eat during the process.

What drives people to work? Apart from the obvious needs of food, shelter and security, what causes people to strive for advancement and achievement, often well beyond the rewards of status or money? Why do people seek to cultivate opportunity: frequently for other people, just as much as for themselves?

Purpose

Professionals who have a strong sense of purpose are usually described as single-minded or focused. Their ability to set a goal and head towards it is what sets them apart and enables the achievement of results. They are initiative-takers, able to prioritise and inwardly motivated to excel. Many organisations seek to hire these types not least because leaders often see themselves in this way, and seek to recruit in their own image. 'Someone like me, about twelve years younger' as one manager summarised his requirements.

People with strong purpose get their courage and energy from achieving their visions or goals, and from being recognised as 'top of the class'. They are not content to coast along with the crowd, and they thrive on a clear sense of direction, which they are perfectly capable of determining for themselves. They thrive on goal-setting and achievement: indeed much of the literature about motivation and performance is designed with these types of people in mind.

Meaning

A different type of professional (equally motivated by purpose and meaning) is the one who is more motivated by *contributing* and is more interested in the meaning of the work than in the 'achievement of a goal or end state'. These are the professionals who lose track of time when fascinated by the task in hand. They enjoy solving problems and/or collaborating with others who are equally attentive to quality work.

Those who attach a strong meaning to their work tend to get their courage and energy from contributing, by knowing what they are doing is somehow valuable and making a difference. Even a vague sense of this is often enough, because they get their courage from a variety of sources, notably mental stimulation, collaboration and the use of their special skills and talents. As long as the work has some value and significance, this often meets their requirements.

On average, people who are driven by meaningful work are the single largest group in the workplace, which we calculate to be about 48 per cent. In many professional organisations they will be even more numerous: particularly in service organisations where expertise lies at the core of the service offering. This group is intrinsically motivated, and extrinsic rewards (even remuneration) don't necessarily motivate them to excel.

Discouraging forces

Most performance programmes are designed to motivate goal-oriented behaviour, which is most accessible to purposeful types. They often rely on extrinsic motivators such as money, ratings or reward systems. However, much of the money (and effort) expended in training, coaching, performance improvement, bonuses and 360-degree feedback is unfortunately wasted on those with a tendency towards finding meaning. Indeed, these contributors can even feel demotivated by such initiatives: their interest lies *intrinsically* in the work, and not *extrinsically* in the adjectives (or targets) attached to it.

The message that many people receive – across organisations both large and small – is 'don't bother us with the detail of what you are doing; just give us the result and meet the deadline. We don't need to know how you got there: too much information!' Not surprisingly, many contributors feel overlooked and ignored.

Every week, we see people being discouraged in all types of organisations and professional firms; often by the very initiatives put in place to 'motivate' them. These include:

- **Incentives and rewards** While these measures work well for those with a strong sense of purpose and achievement, they are more likely to discourage those who derive more satisfaction from the usefulness of their design/solution/ labour. Far from creating a sense of meaning, rewards tend to emphasise the transactional nature of professional activity.
- **Appraisals and feedback** If the feedback received is about the usefulness of work (i.e. how your work is valuable), then this is indeed appreciated by those who are motivated by meaning. If you receive an assessment (or a grading) that refers to how well you performed a task in terms of delivering what you were asked within a deadline (however arbitrary or meaningless the task or deadline is) then this will only motivate if you are goal-oriented and sensitive to achievement.
- **Performance improvement** People who need to find meaning in their work are usually hard-working people. Those who are self-aware will be the first to admit that they may get lost in the problem-solving, in the intrinsic interest in the task. Nevertheless, they resent being 'dumped upon' by people who are task- or goal-focused – particularly if they have not been consulted in advance about the performance- improvements needed.

Did the third stonemason go to work to get a bonus? Or to get good grades in the next review? Or to meet targets? Surely his interest (and hence his courage) came from the *ultimate end-result* of his labour, which he may never even have lived to see. This is what supplied his essential purpose and meaning.

People who find it easiest to access this gateway are those who are able to blend the two elements of purpose and meaning. They have sufficient tendency towards goal-oriented behaviour and achievement, while still able to attach sufficient meaning to what they do. Accordingly, their goals have significance over and above the simple fact of their achievement.

Changing times

Having a strong sense of purpose and meaning can be hard to access when your expertise is in over-supply. Scarcity drives value, and many professionals pride themselves on having specialist skills. When their expertise is diluted by over-supply, the value and meaning of their work decreases... particularly if nobody wants their expertise.

The situation is worsened when there is little positive feedback to reinforce a sense of fulfilment. Demotivation and a feeling of losing your way can start to overwhelm your efforts. You end up wondering 'What's the point?'.

To take just one well-known example: many IT skills have been off-shored to Asia; it is now cheaper to develop software in India than in Europe. So if you are a European software developer, and you now cannot get a job, what does this do to your sense of purpose and meaning?

Karl is a good example of a professional who is coming up against the issue of skill over-supply. He has grown a successful career around project and then programme management in the Netherlands. In the context of his expertise, he is assured and well-regarded. Nevertheless, opportunities are drying up due to projects being cancelled, the commoditisation of project-management skills and the commoditisation of his market.

The significance of purpose and meaning

Karl will need courage to deal with the changes in his marketplace. You may recall we defined courage as 'the capacity to act, in spite of known fears, risks or uncertainty'. In turbulent times, purpose and meaning provide access to courage in three significant ways.

First, purpose provides the volition to act. Setting goals and objectives will make Karl more likely to take action each day. Second, meaning is an important moderator of fear and uncertainty. You can overcome the ups and downs along the way by staying focused on whatever has meaning for you. You can allow the minutiae to flow around you. You have something to 'counterweight' the negative emotions associated with uncertainty and fear.

Third, both purpose and meaning are decided by you, not the world around you, so the locus of control is *inside*. This greatly enhances a feeling of life satisfaction: people who have a strong inner locus of control are more likely to report being happy and contented. They have a higher capacity to act.

So how strong is your sense of meaning and purpose? As we work through each of these seven gateways, may we ask you to rate your sense of purpose as follows:

4 = Excellent, clear and visible even in tough times
3 = Good, though perhaps in need of refinement/upgrade
2 = Vague and/or unclear, perhaps no longer appropriate to my life
1 or 0 = Low, little sense of value in what I do

'Purpose' and 'meaning' are distinct as we have already discussed. We are looking to explore what happens when the two come together. You may find it easier to talk about 'vision': feel free to substitute whatever word works for you, as long as it relates to the future and a sense of the combined strength of purpose and meaning.

While you are deciding, let's hear what our friends have to say.

Adam:
'I just want to get a job, and find my place in the marketplace. I don't have an overarching "world-peace" type of dream. I'm not Martin Luther King. But I know what I want, so let's just say 1.'

Janique:
'I want to give my children the best possible start in life. I still dream of turning this awful situation around, and this is what motivates me to keep sending those CVs late into the evening. So, though I feel a long way from this dream just now, for me this is a 3.'

Maria:

'I feel like a light has been switched on. Even from the short description so far, I really get the distinction between purpose and meaning, and while I am surrounded with "purposes", unfortunately I have lost sight of the "meaning". Staying ahead of the game is so challenging, I've forgotten what the game is.

'I went into HR because I do care about people. But now I'm dealing with whole groups of "resources" and setting policies and procedures for people that I wouldn't even recognise if they walked into this room. So, to be honest, I'm somewhere between a 0 and a 1. I feel very sad to be saying this, but relieved that I know where to start looking.'

Graham:

'I'm having difficulty getting my head around this one. I can certainly picture my being successful again; is this vision of purpose and meaning? If it is, I certainly don't feel it. A bit sceptical about this... Let's say 1.'

Karl:

'No problems for me here. I have a strong sense of purpose, and enjoy bringing order to chaos, so programme management works for me. For me achievement is important, and I can see how developing a sense of purpose gives stability and consistency. Let's call this a 3.'

The future

Whether we call this 'vision', 'purpose', or 'meaning', this gateway to courage is significant for most people. Whatever form it takes, clarity of purpose enables Adam to take actions he would rather avoid. It motivates Karl to continue trying and figure out his business-development problems. It motivates Janique to do her best for her children.

On the other hand, absence of meaning is robbing Maria of her normal brilliance and energy. Beyond the next corporate target, she misses a sense of significance in her work. She is therefore questioning the value of what she is doing and 'something is missing'.

But what about Karl the Confident? So far, he is reporting both a strong sense of connection and a strong sense of purpose. What has he got to learn here?

Purpose and Meaning is a particularly important gateway for those with the following personality characteristics:

1. Openness dimension: Consistent (vs Curious): Those who can sustain routine action benefit from having a clear purpose to do so. They build courage by defining a 'cathedral' and then working consistently, like the stonemason, towards that goal. Of our five friends, who strikes you as consistent?

Both Karl and Adam have shown they can act consistently. Despite setbacks, both are still striving for a goal. Janique is also maintaining a tough daily routine, inspired directly by a sense of purpose around her children.

2. Conscientiousness dimension: Efficient and Organised (vs Easy-going and Spontaneous): People with this characteristic need to have some type of objective, towards which they can organise themselves. Usually they do so quite naturally, but often they outgrow their objectives without realising it. One of our friends perfectly fits this description: who is it?

Like most of the others (except Graham), Maria is very structured and organised. Yet she has clearly outgrown her current sense of meaning and purpose. Maria needs to connect with a sense of meaning in order to get her energy back. Once she does, a lot of other gateways will open/reopen.

3. Extroversion dimension: Solitary (vs Outgoing): Being internally regulated, introverts derive courage from a strong sense of purpose. While extroverts can ignore this gateway, and feed off interaction with others, introverts find the 'inner gateways' particularly useful. Which of our friends fit this description?

Clearly Graham does, but also Adam and perhaps Janique... we simply don't know yet.

4. Agreeableness dimension: Challenging (vs Adaptable): Those who do not rely on social harmony and are able to pursue their own sense of purpose and meaning can find this gateway very accessible. They are free of the need to people-please so they can rely on their inner sense of purpose irrespective of the impact on others. When others naturally fall in step with them, they do well: though they sometimes struggle to co-opt people into a shared vision. Who fits this description most?

Both Graham and Karl are very determined people and both are self-sufficient in their working habits. Graham works a lot in isolation and Karl sets the agenda for his meetings. If they can learn to build a common purpose with others, they can enhance their own sense of purpose by engaging other people in a shared vision that will create opportunity on a wider scale.

5. Neuroticism dimension: Sensitive (vs Assured): These people often suffer from anxiety, and a sense of purpose helps to provide a lighthouse in the storm, a beacon towards which they can navigate. Among our five friends, who would benefit?

Certainly Janique and Graham. Karl also has a fair level of anxiety, but this seems specific to his current situation; one suspects he is normally more assured.

Both Karl and Graham come across as 'Challenging' (low on Agreeableness) and hence may find this gateway particularly accessible. If so, this is fortunate as Purpose and Meaning often helps depressed people like Graham (high on Neuroticism) find a source of strength and a capacity for action.

While many of our friends may get benefit via the Purpose and Meaning gateway, Janique is already finding it invaluable. Maria knows she has work to do here: to find new perspective and a new sense of meaning. Graham will also find it useful at some point, though he has difficulty seeing this just yet.

Exercise

You have already scored this gateway in terms of how you feel about it. Now score this again, based on your personality characteristics: High, Medium or Low?

Top tips to help you develop Purpose and Meaning

1. Articulating your personal vision Finding meaning comes from having a sense of who you are, what you stand for and pursing activities that align to these thoughts (either as an individual or in creating a brand). Knowing what you stand for can be tough. Articulating a personal vision, or a shared vision in the case of a team or group of people, is central to cultivating opportunities for meaningful work. There are lots of exercises out there for developing personal vision. One of our favourites is in the *Fifth Discipline Handbook* by Peter Senge (Drawing Forth Personal Vision). You can benefit from investing time and headspace in such exercises.

2. Finding new ways of dealing with setbacks When faced with perceived failure, it's useful to try to make sense of things that have gone wrong and find meaning to deal with the uncomfortable emotions that accompany setbacks. Can you remove all blame from the equation? Can you get curious about causes and influences? Can you place yourself in the shoes of an observer, and see events from a different perspective?

3. Move from 'problem solving' to a 'solution-focused' approach. Solution-focused approaches cultivate opportunity by disengaging from the problem and developing a strong sense of positive purpose. The approach requires you to:
   · Identify a preferred outcome and orientate towards this goal (keep track and refine);
   · Disengage from problem-focused thinking, towards 'What if?', accepting setbacks as part of the creative process);
   · Identify and activate the resources and strengths required to achieve your goal.

12

Third Gateway – Influence and Communication Skill

'Think twice before you speak, because your words and influence will plant the seed of either success or failure in the mind of another' – Napoleon Hill

Successful people know that a good idea is only the start of success. Getting others 'on board' usually takes a lot more time and energy.

The ability to communicate ideas to others, to engage them in a shared understanding and to influence them into action are all essential ingredients of success and opportunity. The stronger your sense of vision, the more you know your strengths, the greater your sense of achievement... the more essential it is to be able to communicate and influence people with your ideas.

If you cannot get others on board, what happens? Unless you can communicate your ideas and influence people to act upon them, you are simply left with thoughts and daydreams – often leading to a deep sense of frustration, disappointment and missed opportunity.

Influence and Communication Skill is a combination of interpersonal skills such as empathy, our ability to engage in dialogue, listening, positive self-presentation and assertiveness techniques. By adapting and modifying our personal style when we become aware of the effect we have on other people, we are able to access courage through this gateway and cultivate opportunity.

This gateway reinforces courage by cultivating skills such as asking, and increasing the likelihood of getting a positive response. This in turn makes it more likely that you will ask again, and your capacity to act is therefore enlarged.

If you know you can communicate and influence others, you are stronger in your belief about yourself. If you can listen, present ideas and engage others, you already have a sense of personal power.

Frustration

Sheer force of will is not enough; indeed it may spell frustration or discouragement. If a professional does not also possess the ability to communicate, their talents and ideas may remain hidden. The vision may fail to engage others, and hence may never be realised. The understanding of good friends may be appreciated, but to cultivate opportunity, Influence and Communication Skill is a must.

It's deeply frustrating for talented people to see others succeeding when they are not. Those who seem to get ahead are not always the brightest, the best qualified or have the best ideas. How often does an intelligent person find themselves in an audience – at work, or watching TV – thinking, 'I could do better than that'? They experience both frustration and discouragement at the same time.

To understand the link between communication skill and courage, it is perhaps easiest to see what happens when communication skill is *absent,* or not as well developed as other talents. Frustration is just one possible result. But there are others: such as resentment towards others who fail to recognise one's special abilities. This can lead to feelings of being invisible, ignored or insignificant which may result in diminishing confidence in one's self and creeping doubt about one's own abilities. A build-up of these negative emotions often leads to withdrawal, a retreat into a safe space which ultimately diminishes one's ability to act.

The tragedy is that, in many cases, problems of communication can be more easily corrected than problems in other areas. Communication skills can be learned. It may take some uncomfortable feedback and honest effort, but new habits can be formed. As long as the professional is willing to do the work, the support of competent professionals can speed up the process. The basic shifts can usually be made in a few weeks, and even the more refined ones can be learned over a few months.

To take a common example, some clever people simply talk too much. They go into 'their story' far too quickly, and spend too long telling it. In doing so, they fail to notice that others have switched off, lost interest or are just nodding out of politeness. This common error stems from not grasping that communication is more about active listening than active talking. Developing and honing listening skills thereby increases the ability to sense and interpret what is required.

At the opposite extreme, an introvert may not speak enough. They may wait to be consulted, or for the 'right time' to state their ideas. They may retreat into a mania of 'preparation', constantly postponing the moment of interaction with others. In search of perfect communication, they end up doing no communication at all.

Common pitfalls

Other common mistakes include...

- Starting a discussion with too much detail about themselves, their 'story' or their 'pitch'
- Focusing too quickly on the *content* of their expertise, as opposed to the *context* in which these skills might be valuable
- Sitting passively in meetings, not letting their voice be heard until they are asked
- Accepting the agenda of others, making no effort to influence the programme
- Ignoring body language that indicates others have lost interest
- Being too accommodating, being taken for granted via the inability to say No
- Talking too much, solving problems about which nobody cares, trying to prove how clever they are
- Waiting to speak instead of listening to what is being said and directing the response to answer the questions posed
- Allowing others to interrupt them, being unable to set boundaries and 'push-back'

Given the impact both on courage and opportunity, one would imagine that these issues would be swiftly put right. The problem is that the person is often *unaware* of the issue, at least consciously. They are at the stage of 'unconscious incompetence' and hence it's hard for learning to begin. When confronted with issues of appearance, communication or personal organisation, many react by self-justification. 'That's just not my style', 'Others don't think so', 'That was an isolated case because of...', 'Clients expect that...', 'But the detail is important!', etc.

It seems we can be very precious about our habits of communication, and we do not like it when these are criticised or challenged. Even when we want to learn, we can be reluctant to change. Or we lack some essential ingredient to do so.

Indeed, the immediate effect of feedback can be *discouraging*, rather than encouraging. Even when feedback is well delivered as observation (and often it's not, but is delivered as judgemental adjectives or ratings), the immediate effect may be disappointment, annoyance and a sense of rejection.

Crucial shift

How we communicate is very personal. What we say is the public display or window on our inner world and personality. It therefore takes courage to change the way we communicate, to learn new influencing skills. But these skills are a gateway to courage. Being a skilled communicator makes asking easier.

Learning communication skills means putting the ego aside in order to become a student for a while. It requires an openness to new approaches and possibilities, in situations where as yet we don't have evidence of success. It means tolerating the risks that it might go wrong, for the simple reason that in the domain of communication skills, nothing works all the time. It's an art as much as a science.

Yet the rewards are significant. The ability to learn communication skills enhances one's strength in dialogue, and this builds courage. This allows a professional to gain trust and discover vital information; essential preludes to cultivating opportunity both for oneself and for other people.

One simple benefit often reported early on is, '*At least I didn't react when s/he said...*' It's impossible to influence a conversation if one is pre-programmed to react. Influence is the ability to take a conversation in a different direction. If we are stuck in react mode, we simply don't have the communication skill to influence opportunity.

The ability to communicate enhances courage by making a professional more capable of engaging with others, and hence influencing the course of their lives. Even in the face of setback and disappointment, these skills enable a professional to overcome disempowering habits such as reaction or retreat.

Let's explore a couple of 'cornerstone skills': listening and asking.

Listening

Before we explore asking, we need to explore listening. Listening is a key part of communication skill because it enables us to ask the right questions. Listening skills are arguably the cornerstone of good communication and influencing. Listening is one of the most important skills you can have. How well you listen has a major impact on your job effectiveness, and on the quality of your relationships with others. We listen to obtain information. We listen to understand. We listen for enjoyment. We listen to learn.

However, listening does not come naturally to most people. Many of us need to work hard to stop ourselves 'jumping in' and giving opinions. Mostly, people don't listen – they just take turns to speak. Depending on the study being quoted, we remember between 25 per cent and 50 per cent of what we hear. That means that when we talk to our boss, colleagues, customers or spouse for ten minutes, they probably pay attention to less than half of the conversation.

By becoming a better listener, we improve our productivity, as well as our ability to influence, persuade and negotiate. We avoid conflict and misunderstandings. When we are understood we feel affirmed and validated and we achieve more.

There are different types of listening. Typically they are presented as levels of listening. The higher up the list our friends can get, the better communicators and influencers they will become. If they can reach the level of active listening they will see great improvements in their ability to access courage.

1. **Passive listening/not listening** – noise in background – basically ignoring (typical in open-plan offices)
2. **Pretend listening** – also called 'responsive listening' – using stock nods and smiles and uhum, yes, of course, etc.
3. **Biased/projective listening** – 'selective listening' and intentionally disregarding/dismissing the other person's views
4. **Misunderstood listening** – unconsciously overlaying your own interpretations and making things fit when they don't
5. **Attentive listening** – personally driven fact gathering and analysis often with manipulation of the other person
6. **Active listening** – understanding feelings and gathering facts for largely personal purposes
7. **Empathic listening** – understanding and checking facts and feelings, usually to listener's personal agenda
8. **Facilitative listening** – listening, understanding fully, and helping, with the other person's needs uppermost

Empathy is required to listen well. Empathy is the ability to experience and relate to the thoughts, emotions, or experience of others. Empathy is more than simple sympathy, which is being able to understand and support others with compassion or sensitivity.

Empathy is positively related to job performance, according to many studies including a recent white paper by the Centre for Creative Leadership. Fortunately, empathy is not a fixed trait. It can be learned (Shapiro, 2002[3]). If given enough time and support, our friends can develop and enhance their empathy skills through coaching, training, or developmental opportunities and initiatives.

Asking

If you have listened well, you will have a deep sense of the other's needs, so you will be able to ask powerful questions. These will enhance your capacity to influence and guide the actions of other people. If you can shape a conversation where the other person is equally engaged, your courage will be enhanced in the process.

---

3. Shapiro, Johanna *PhDAcademic Medicine*, April 2002, Volume 77 (4), pp 323–328.

When a good dialogue occurs about a difficult subject, even the differences create a deep sense of understanding. You leave such a conversation with renewed confidence in your capacity to act... and this is the essence of courage.

A conversation is usually directed by the questions posed. When someone says 'What shall we talk about?' or 'What bothers you most about this problem?' or 'Can you help me with...', they are guiding and shaping the dialogue, and the relationship between the people in the dialogue. Furthermore, asking questions is a powerful way of conveying your point of view, and discovering the other person's assumptions and perspectives.

As well as solving problems, a well-formulated question has the effect of opening up new channels of thinking and removing blocks to progress. In this way, it builds good relationships, trust and rapport. In client situations, questions can clarify issues, open up new areas of discussion and close sales.

Examples of courageous questions:

- 'Would you be willing to help me with something?' (request, may be refused)
- 'Why does that keep happening?' (may uncover uncomfortable truth)
- 'What do you really want?' (may put the other on the spot)
- 'Can we meet to discuss this further?' (request, could end in rejection)
- 'Why do you need to do that?' (challenging assumptions)

You will notice how some of these questions may well result in rejection. This is precisely what makes them courageous. If there is no risk, the issue of courage is irrelevant.

Once you start to link listening and asking skills together you can start to create influence. Truly masterful influencing skill requires a healthy combination of interpersonal skills (such as empathy), communication skills (such as listening), presentation and assertiveness techniques. By adapting and modifying their personal style when they become aware of the effect they are having on other people, our friends can access the courage to ask.

To a greater or lesser extent, all our five friends need to do some learning about communication skills. Whether they know it or not, their skills need an 'upgrade' to deal with an evolving world. In a moment, we will see how they see it; but first, what about you?

How well would you rate your own ability to influence? Thinking about the space in which you would like to create opportunity (whether for yourself or others), would you say your ability to communicate is:

4 = Excellent, e.g. able to shift any agenda, and bring others along with you

3 = Good, every day gives me opportunities to learn and refine

2 = Don't know, I may be stuck in habits that I'm unaware of. But I think it's OK

1 or 0 = Low, I lack confidence and ability in this area.

As a rule of thumb, you may have to make allowances for certain natural tendencies. If your tendency is towards confidence, you may overstate the positive feedback you believe you are getting. On the other hand, if you currently feel very discouraged, it is equally possible to overstate how awful you are at influencing others. So you may need to mark-up or mark-down to allow for your mood or tendency.

In the end however, you need to believe your own score. Let's hear what our friends have to say.

Adam:
'It's a 1. I know I have lots to learn here. I'm keen to find out what this is, and get on with it. Personally, I don't have any problem being a student in this area, and taking feedback. I just need to know that it will be worth it, and get results. How am I coming across?'

Janique:
'Like Adam, it's a 1. I probably need to completely reformulate my approach to the job market in Paris. At the moment, I'm surviving but I want more. I'm prepared to believe this will entail a complete rewrite of my entire self-presentation, CV, story… maybe even style and appearance! But I do think I am an empathic person, so there is some hope.'

Maria:
'In this space, I don't feel too bad. I am able to build consensus and also to shape an agenda. Sure, I have things to learn: don't we all? It's a 3.'

Karl:
'Right, this is where I need to go to work. I felt very uncomfortable when you talked about "unconscious incompetence" because I suspect that's exactly where I am. I'm not building consensus in the way Maria has just mentioned. I probably am shaping the agenda, but perhaps a bit too much. I didn't even know empathy was part of this so that says a lot. Definitely need to explore this further... Let's say a 1.'

Graham:
'Yes, I've been schooled in the techniques of communication, but I wouldn't say it comes naturally. I'm not great in social situations, and small-talk bores me. I would like to do some learning here. So I was going to say 2, but took your advice about adjusting for mood, so I need the courage to say a 1.'

The courage to ask questions

So what questions might each of our friends ask, in order to open doors and create opportunity?

Karl:
'Before we start today's meeting, can I just ask for your input on something?'

Janique:
'I know we have not spoken for months, but may I ask for your advice?'

Graham:
'Hannah, can we take a half-hour to brainstorm a few ideas to pull in more clients?'

Karl:
'Over the past year, what has been the single greatest evolution in how you manage programmes?'

Graham:
'Who else should I talk to?'

Janique:
'What are the implications for consumer marketing?'

These questions take a certain amount of courage, but the communication skill to ask them also *creates* courage. (And opportunity.) Even while we are refining the questions, we learn on the journey. With the help of others, we eventually find out what we need to know, provided we are able to 'hear the answers' as they truly are rather than as we want them to be.

The courage to make requests

Questions in turn lead to requests. Empathic skills help us to make appropriate requests, if we have the courage to do so. For Karl, Janique, Graham and indeed all of our friends, their understanding of the other person's world or perspective is vital to making requests that will help each of them get a positive response and build their courage further... for example...

Karl:
'Would you be willing to take part in a short piece of research?'

Janique:
'Jean-Marc, if I were to rewrite my CV following this conversation, would you be willing to review it with me, again by phone?'

Graham:
'Would you be willing to introduce us?'

Karl:
'In order to do that proposal, we will need to spend a couple of hours together. Are we both willing to invest this time?'

Graham:
'If we could organise a three-way lunch, would you be willing to come along and talk about why you are introducing us?'

Janique:
'I see from LinkedIn you have good connections in Coca-Cola. Would you be willing to forward my CV?'

Whatever the outcome, these are the types of requests in which our friends need to become fluent. It takes courage to practise these things, but asking also builds courage and opportunity. This is the central thesis of this book.

Influence and Communication skill is a particularly important gateway for those with the following personality characteristics:

1. **Openness dimension: All:** Curious people are naturally open to experience, they have a natural advantage in deploying their innate curiosity in conversation. Curious people tend to be good at asking, while Consistent people are often good at listening. Who will be good at asking, and who will be better at listening?

Both Graham and Maria are naturally curious, so both should find asking easy. Karl (though more Consistent than Curious) is likely to derive a lot of benefit from switching from 'tell mode' to 'ask mode'. Adam needs to increase his level of interaction, and Janique feels she has no room for interaction.

2. **Conscientiousness dimension: All:** Organised and efficient people will be organised in their communication and questioning, while easy-going people tend to do this spontaneously. This personality characteristic does not preclude anyone from accessing this gateway, but the way they do so will be different.

3. **Extroversion dimension: Outgoing (vs Solitary)**: This is an obvious gateway for extroverts, and communication skill adds to their talent with other people and so builds their courage. One of the five has a naturally outgoing personality, but is not making the most of this. Who and why?

Karl is naturally outgoing and has no difficulty meeting people. Yet because he is stuck in 'tell mode', he is not yet making the most of this gateway, and accordingly is experiencing a lot of frustration.

4. **Agreeableness dimension: Adaptable (vs Challenging)**: When those with high 'Agreeableness' can couple this with good Influence and Communication Skills, they tend to win the trust of others both rapidly and deeply. At least three of our friends will be able to do this, indeed one of them already is. Who are they?

Adam and Janique both score high on Agreeableness, and when they sharpen their communication skills as well, this will enhance their sense of courage. Maria already possesses good communication skills, as well as the experience of using them. She probably wins trust... but does she trust others?

5. **Neuroticism dimension: Assured (vs Sensitive)**: Those who don't experience emotional 'highs and lows' have a slight advantage with this gateway because their mood is more consistent, and hence they can more consistently apply communication skills. Who would be good examples of this?

Maria, Adam and Karl all possess a fair degree of Assurance, and so should find this gateway fairly easily. They won't feel too embarrassed when practising new social skills. Being more sensitive, Graham and Janique may find this harder.

Top tips to help you Influence and Communicate

1. Learning how to listen Use the listening levels in the chapter and test yourself. How do you listen most of the time? Set yourself a realistic goal to improve your listening. Start with a specific person or event in mind, such as a meeting. A quick win bearing immediate reward would be to start with your spouse, partner or children. What difference is this making? What have you noticed that you may have missed before?

2. Developing the skill of empathy Empathic skills can be enhanced by putting time aside to give time and attention to others – especially when you are under time pressure (if you really want to stretch yourself). When you hear yourself criticising people, you are seeing things from your point of view, not from theirs. Stop, take a moment and consider a different perspective. Cultivate the compassionate voice inside. Watching empathy in action is another good way of learning the skill. You might think about how a certain person you consider empathic might respond in a situation, or watching family interactions between a patient parent and a child can also be very useful. Studies taking mothers and babies into schools and workplaces show that the more you observe empathy in action, the better you become at 'feeling' it and being able to replicate it.

3. Increasing influence by building your credibility Enhancing your credibility with others is one of the best ways to become more influential. People want to follow the advice and counsel of those with expertise, and you want to be one of those people. It is not enough to be an expert on a subject matter or a situation. You must also be *perceived* as an expert. That perception comes from how you carry yourself and interact with others. Credibility is a combination of expertise and trustworthiness. Kevin Hogan, in *The Science of Influence*, states it as a formula: Credibility = Expertise + Trustworthiness. (See Chapter 10 for tips on building trust.)

13
Fourth Gateway
– Self-awareness

'He who knows others is wise. He who knows himself is enlightened' – Lao Tzu (Chinese Taoist philosopher, founder of Taoism)

So far, we have explored three gateways to courage: Connection to Others, Purpose and Meaning and Influence and Communication Skill, particularly the power of asking. We now move on to the fourth gateway that enables people to access courage: greater self-awareness, particularly of their own strengths.

Self-awareness is having a clear perception of your personality, including strengths, weaknesses, thoughts, beliefs, motivation and emotions. It allows you to understand other people, how they perceive you, your attitude and your responses to them in the moment. With that understanding you have a better chance of engaging with them and creating opportunity.

Self-awareness theory states that when we focus our attention on ourselves, we evaluate and compare our current behaviour to our internal standards and values. Various emotional states are intensified by self-awareness. People are more likely to align their behaviour with their standards when made self-aware. For some people, this will be negatively affected if they don't live up to their personal standards. For others it will increase their sense of authenticity and volition.

Self-awareness may conjure up miserable memories of being given 'feedback' at appraisal time or being told what you're not very good at. Indeed many organisations and individuals reflect only on the things they wish to improve. It's perhaps not a surprise to hear that many people resist reflecting on their strengths. Increasing self-awareness and focusing on strengths, however, can unleash potential and help cultivate opportunity.

Sometimes this is countercultural – for example, perhaps 'it's not the done thing to brag'. Other times it's because self-awareness in organisational terms has been driven by an agenda of competencies and bringing everyone up to an acceptable level across a broad base of skills, knowledge and behaviours rather than playing to and promoting people's strengths. Added to this is the problem that deep down, many of us don't believe we possess any special talents or abilities at all. So you may look at this gateway with doubt, suspecting that if it leads anywhere at all, it will just be a muddy track to a wasteland overgrown with weeds. Take heed, self-awareness is more about understanding your strengths and talents than it is about knowing your weaknesses.

The link to courage

The gateway of self-awareness helps access courage by allowing people to identify their strengths and use those strengths to positive effect. In doing so, they do more of it, because a positive feedback loop is created: by using our strengths we come to rely on them.

For example, if someone knows they are a good listener, they will do more listening and therefore they will hear more. In this way, they will have more information upon which to base their decisions and actions. They trust their ability to gather relevant information, and to have a realistic view of themselves. This enhances courage.

The ability to pinpoint your strengths and to use these to capitalise on situations is what drives the courage to ask. Developing a self-awareness of your strengths allows you to start asking in those areas in which you are most likely to succeed. This builds a self-fulfilling cycle of positive energy and confidence growth.

A person's recent experience can however cloud the picture. For example, in the months following redundancy, failure of investment, disappointing sales or the loss of key team members, a person may doubt even their most cherished beliefs about their own strengths. Whatever talents they thought they had may simply appear as illusory. 'If I really was so talented in this area, how could that have happened?'

Few people lie awake at night wondering about their strengths. One person worries that their technical or communication skills may be going out of date. Another lies awake wondering if they will be able to lead that team that they are suddenly leading. Another fears conflict, and the very thought of that meeting in tomorrow's agenda fills them with dread.

Yet, recent preliminary research quoted in *International Coaching Psychology Review* suggests that if we did lie awake thinking more about our strengths, we are more likely to report being happy! Strength-spotting appears to correlate with happiness and can be used as an effective intervention to promote happier living.

What do we focus on?

So why do we focus on our weaknesses more naturally than on our strengths? Before we start berating ourselves too much, it's perhaps worthwhile to note that most of us have, to some extent, been educated to think in this way. If your mum went to a parent-teacher meeting and was told that you were excellent at languages, superb at music but had some difficulty with maths, what was the subject of conversation when she came home? In what domain were you asked to pay more attention? If additional tuition were to be engaged, would that be for languages or for maths?

We have been focusing on our weaknesses for a very long time. When looking at the future, risk generally tends to have more weight than opportunity. It's hardly surprising that work often turns into a constant striving to compensate for things that we are *not* very good at.

Yet it pays to focus on strengths. No matter how low one is feeling, accessing a sense of special ability or talent renews energy, gives hope for the future and raises self-esteem in the present. Even when dealing with criticism or rejection, it is possible to tap an inner resource no matter how negative others are being about us.

'You are the only person on earth who can use your ability' – Zig Zigler

Magnifying glass

What we focus on gets bigger. The more we think about risk and weakness, the greater it gets. Our minds do not just passively analyse the world around us, our minds are active agents in creating it.

Take someone who is obsessed with money: they will be trying to cut costs, and grasping every opportunity that comes their way. Their fear of financial loss may be keeping them awake at night. Their mind resembles a calculator or a spreadsheet, constantly re-calculating money.

So when they meet someone for the first time, they are often sizing that person up as a potential customer, or perhaps a cheaper source of supply, or of labour. If the former, they may be exploring who they know and how that can wangle an introduction. If the latter, they will be sizing up just how desperate the other person is, so that they can engage their services at the least possible cost.

The conversation that results will reflect their mindset. Often their body language will, too. When the bill comes in a restaurant, their behaviour may also betray their concern with money, for example by being hesitant to pay, or even too quick to pay. Consciously or subconsciously, other people will notice and conduct themselves accordingly. In hundreds of ways every day, our mindsets actively create the world we inhabit.

Much the same applies to how we think about ourselves. If people are obsessed with their weaknesses, this will be evident both in tone of voice and in what they say. They may speak about themselves in self-deprecating ways. They may be constantly searching for courses, books and specialists. They may express worry, doubt, or concern about risk. Even when not speaking, their body language will probably be protective and unsure.

Thought patterns are massively important when it comes to courage. Our magnifying-glass minds will be operating; using either **en**couraging or **dis**couraging stories about the past, optimistic or pessimistic images about the future. We are actively creating the world in which we live: to a degree that few people can imagine. But thought patterns are not set within us. We can unlearn them and learn more positive ways of thinking instead. Once we have identified negative thinking patterns through becoming self-aware, we are able to change them. Our thinking patterns dictate how we subsequently feel, so if we change how we think, we change how we feel.

If we want courage to grow, it's vital that we learn the skills of self-reflection and focus on our strengths, not on our weaknesses. Self-awareness requires compassion for the self and willingness to believe in the good in oneself (that is, your strengths) in order to be a force for positive change.

What's your story?

We will be hearing from our five friends in a moment. Before we do so, what is your story? What narrative are you using about yourself, with yourself?

What are your strengths? If asked what your special talents are, how would you reply? What is your special ability? What can you do without much effort? What do others tend to say about you? With what level of conviction are you answering this question?

In short, how would you rate your belief in your talents?

4 =   *High, I know what my talents are, and I see the evidence for this*

3 =   *Good, though sometimes I lose sight of this gateway*

2 =   *Unclear, I know they are there, but lack clarity about what they are. Or evidence.*

1 or 0 =   *Low, deep-down, I don't believe I possess anything particularly special.*

It's the conviction that counts here. You may have read books and done countless exercises about talent development, but what is asked here is your gut-level assurance that these are real for you. Many people have studied talents in an abstract way, and can talk about various scales and books on the subject. But when it comes to their own conviction about themselves, they possess less belief than an amateur dabbler.

Adam:

'I know I have a gift for systems and technology. My computer science degree was not an accidental choice; I have a talent in this area. I'm also pretty good at learning, and I'm not scared by what I don't know.

'I guess I was starting to lose sight of this, until now. When you mentioned recent experience creating doubt, well, that's me. Still, it's a fairly confident 3.'

Janique:
'Recent experience has been so devastating that I'm having difficulty getting beyond this. Yet deep down I know there is something there, and that's why I'm not content to carry on forever with the job I have. So I'm going for a 2, though perhaps a bit surprised to hear myself saying this.'

Maria:
'If you had asked me a year ago, I would have said 4 and meant it. But this sense of something missing is creating real doubt: not just a symptom of lack of confidence. I have talents, for sure, but I'm a long way from being certain about their use. Like Janique, I'm going for a 2.'

Karl:
'I have a clear sense of talent in the context of being a programme-manager, so in that domain it would be a 3. But I simply don't know about my ability to cultivate opportunity. I have to admit that I've not been too successful recently. So there is lack of clarity there – so I'm going to say 2. Like Janique, a bit surprised to hear myself saying this, but for opposite reasons.'

Graham:
'Over the past few years, my situation has been tough: divorce, financial difficulty, clients dropping off the radar. This leaves me feeling quite depressed, and so I find it hard to answer the question. Any number I would give would not be real.'

Strengths-based courage

Ideally our friends will go on to identify their strengths more specifically; there are many helpful books and online tools in this area to help them. Doing so will reinforce their courage and enhance their resilience in the face of a changing world. If Graham can let himself do this, he might find some numbers he can believe in.

It's interesting how conviction about special talent is not necessarily related to experience. Of all our friends, Adam is the youngest, yet he has the highest scores. He knows where his talents lie, even though the marketplace has not yet vindicated his conviction. This is the power of knowing one's talents: it gives a sense of strength even when the immediate circumstances are not favourable, even when there might not yet be evidence to support that assessment.

When self-awareness is focused on strengths, this builds self-belief and courage. When it comes to courage, this is the type of 'inalienable conviction' that we are looking for. The fire glows within, whatever the climate outside the door. No matter how disappointing today was, no matter how indifferent the marketplace, we are warmed by a sense of being special. We can value ourselves and our abilities, whether others choose to value us or not. That's a real gateway to courage.

Gratitude and appreciation of self

This level of strengths-based awareness is usually accompanied by a strong sense of gratitude. It is practically impossible to have a powerful understanding of your strengths and not feel appreciative of yourself. Indeed, if you don't feel some level of appreciation, then your strength inventory may be just an abstract conceptual one, with no sense of conviction that it's real for you. It's a good test.

And gratitude builds courage. Just as complaining robs a person of the power (and energy) to influence their world for the better, gratitude generates positive feelings that move one beyond fear, resentment or uncertainty. You can easily prove this for yourself by doing a fifteen-minute stocktake of those things you appreciate about yourself. What does that do for your courage?

When you are appreciative of yourself, you start to access the reality of your resources: talents, means, friends, loved ones, motivation and, most of all, health. As the list lengthens – and deepens – you can almost feel the courage level rise.

Self-awareness is a particularly useful gateway for those with the following personality characteristics:

1. **Openness dimension: Curious (vs Consistent)**: Curiosity fuels the desire to know more about the self as much as the external world or other things. Those of our friends who possess high levels of curiosity are likely to be more self-aware around their strengths. Who fits this description?

Maria clearly has developed a lot of self-awareness. Even when struggling to identify what is missing, she is open to learning. Graham is falling into the classic trap of blaming his situation instead of using his strengths to see what he can do about it. If someone could challenge him, and tap into his natural curiosity, this might make a big difference.

2. Conscientiousness dimension: Efficient and Organised (vs Easy-going and Spontaneous): People who are more conscientious are more likely to covet self-knowledge than those who are happier to go with the flow. The conscientious mind likes to order things and have knowledge – self-knowledge is therefore seen as a further tool to be better at life – a driving force for the conscientious.

3. Extroversion dimension: All: Both outgoing and solitary people find self-awareness in different ways. Outgoing people are more likely to ask for feedback, while solitary people tend to introspect, read and self-analyse.

4. Agreeableness dimension Adaptable (vs Challenging): Sceptical and challenger types are good at knowing what they want and so have a level of self-awareness. However, they are often unable to override destructive or antagonistic behaviours for the greater good. Implicit in our definition of self-awareness is the desire to relate to others positively in order to create opportunity. Those with more adaptive behaviour styles usually find this gateway easier to access. Which of our friends is adaptable?

Janique has seen huge change and is aware that she has potential. Despite his lack of experience, Adam also has a strong sense of his own strengths and comes across as friendly and adaptable. Both of them should be able to make good use of this gateway; indeed their scores indicate they already are.

5. Neuroticism dimension: All, favouring mid-scores: Both 'assured' and 'sensitive' people can use this gateway, yet those who don't experience emotional 'highs and lows' have a slight advantage in that they will probably use it more consistently. Those at the extreme ends of the spectrum may have the most difficulty. Who, for example?

Of all our friends, Karl may find this hardest because he is highly 'assured'. Being the thickest-skinned and the most confident, he may be the least 'realistically' self-aware.

Top tips to help you develop Self-awareness

1. Developing your inner compassionate self so that the awareness you seek is of the things you do well. When you hear your critical voice, develop your compassionate voice to run an alternative caring perspective. If it helps, imagine what you would say to a young child or a friend who was feeling down. A compassionate voice is an encouraging one.

2. Becoming your own expert. Self-awareness is developed through practising focusing your attention on the details of your personality and behaviour. Think about how you are feeling more often throughout the day. Stop what you are doing. Ask yourself 'how do I feel?', reflect on the answer and record your thoughts. Do this frequently and watch your ability to know how you are feeling and what's going on increase.

3. Identifying your strengths:
- Strengths are present when we persist in our behaviour even though things don't go smoothly.
- Think of a time you have been really successful... describe what happened in detail. What obstacles did you have to overcome?
- Look specifically for any behaviour where you persevered despite obstacles. Ask yourself: what qualities did I show in the face of these obstacles? Do I do this on a regular basis?
- Start by being specific – think about specific behaviours, thoughts and feelings – then summarise these into a more general 'strength'.
- If you find yourself negating your strengths, play devil's advocate with yourself. Examine your dismissals – present the counter argument. Remember, this is a thinking exercise

– challenge your beliefs about yourself. Remember – what we focus on gets bigger – focus on just the strengths.

4. Asking for frequent feedback focusing only on things others think you did well. Check it against the strengths you have identified above. Start to build a log of your talents – look for patterns and themes.

14
Fifth Gateway – Self-discipline

'Because of their size, parents may be difficult to discipline properly' – P. J. O'Rourke

In the last chapter we talked about self-awareness. Self-discipline is linked to self-awareness in that if self-awareness is the knowing, then self-discipline is the doing.

Self-discipline can be defined as the ability to motivate ourselves in spite of a negative emotional state. If you are doing something you enjoy, the motivation is intrinsically generated and self-discipline is not required. Qualities associated with self-discipline include willpower, hard work and persistence. It transcends willpower because whereas willpower is the strength and ability to carry out a certain task, self-discipline is the ability to use willpower routinely, even automatically. Viewed another way, we can define self-discipline as being self-respect, turned into positive action.

Why self-discipline is a gateway to courage

Self-discipline starts with the ability to control our impulses. Once we have impulse-control we are in a better position to think through our responses and choose how we react to things rather than being at the mercy of our emotional triggers.

Some may struggle with the words 'self-discipline'. This may be a legacy of school experiences with rules and regulations, or a puritanical upbringing from which they have rebelled. Nevertheless, the basic human skill of controlling our responses and being disciplined to achieve – even when things are tough, or immediate gratification is absent – is indeed a powerful gateway for creating opportunity. This is because self-discipline can be described as 'the power to act on ideas', the bridge from thought to action.

Self-discipline gives us the capacity to motivate ourselves to get the job done and resist distractions. It is the ability to take things from thoughts and realise them through actions and tangible results. For example, creating a perfect system for processing and organising your emails efficiently is not going to create opportunity until you can make yourself do it whenever you check your email.

Knowledge itself is only part of the path – the path we discussed in our last chapter on self-awareness. Implementation, however, is the step that creates courage and opportunity – and implementation requires self-discipline.

We all exercise degrees of control and discipline. However, when faced with disappointment in ourselves we may 'let things go' and even let ourselves go. Good habits of eating and exercise get eroded by lack of self-care because we don't care or we don't feel worthy of looking after ourselves. The disposition towards action, the ability to make things happen that we once seemed to possess now seems impossible to summon up. This can in turn lead to a withdrawal from connection with others, and other gateways start to close.

With the notion of self-discipline comes the issue of control. A key part of working with self-discipline – and indeed improving it – is understanding the concept of controlling the controllables. Setting unrelenting standards where you have no control of outcomes is not what we mean by self-discipline. Implicit in the notion of self-discipline is the concept of realism. Being realistic builds courage by building on success. As with sports psychology, a key part of developing courage by accessing self-discipline is training yourself to identify and strengthen what is controllable, such as motivation, concentration and distraction control.

Having focus is a fundamental part of self-discipline and central to improving performance. Focus encompasses the skill of concentration; which can be seen as the ability to attend only to what is relevant and to stay dedicated for the duration of the task.

Second, focus encompasses the ability to switch: to shift focus as required by the task or changing conditions. When our focus starts to drift (as opposed to shift) from the process – whether to outcomes or to what others think, for example – we can fall into the trap of procrastination, poor judgement and, ultimately, bad decisions.

The enemy of focus and self-discipline in today's society is multitasking. Although often held up as a critical strength and in certain circumstances (such as being a working parent) clearly a necessity, distractions and a lack of focus impede our ability to succeed. For example, thinking too much about an impending deadline or the eventual outcome often leads to mistakes or increases anxiety that impairs best focus.

Hutchinson's Law states: Any occurrence requiring undivided attention will be accompanied by an equally compelling distraction. What sets courageous people apart is their ability to maintain focus in the face of challenges, setbacks and distractions, and critically to get back on track quickly if losing focus. Everyone gets distracted; it's the speed and ability to get back on track that constitutes self-discipline.

Accessing the gateway of self-discipline allows us to (i) accept what has happened, (ii) plan an alternative response and (iii) implement the response. The ability to recognise when we are sidetracked or becoming concerned with the minutiae of a problem all stem from our self-discipline. The motto of the self-disciplined with regard to focus is 'Be here now'.

What's your story?

We will be hearing from our five friends in a moment. Before we do so, what is your relationship with self-discipline? How well can you maintain focus?

4 = High: I concentrate well, do what I plan to do, I am quick to refocus as required

3 = Good, though sometimes I may drift and enjoy the distraction

2 = Mixed, I know I should be focused, but I'm not. Don't always do what's on my list

1 or 0 = Easily distracted, I go with the flow and see where things take me

Adam:
'This is a crucial gateway for me. Recently, I've been getting up late and not doing what I know I should be doing. There seems to be no focus to my activities; they would best be described as random. So it's a 1.'

Janique:
'I score high here, a 4. I have to, but I recognise that I'm often multitasking. I'm very focused on the here and now and I do what needs to be done. What I need is a longer-term strategy to get me out of my current situation. I can access this gateway easily, and it gives me courage, what I need to do is use it to open other gateways.'

Maria:
'I am focused and disciplined. This has worked well in the past, when I've known what I wanted. The problem is that I need to shift focus, and I don't yet know how or where. A 2.'

Karl:
'I am very ordered and disciplined and can access this gateway easily. It's a 4.'

Graham:
'What discipline? It's just not a word that features in my vocabulary or my life. I don't want to become regimented or boring or back at school. I don't like being told what to do even by myself. This gateway is about as attractive as the school gateway was. A zero.'

The significance of Self-discipline

'The nicest thing about not planning is that failure comes as a complete surprise, rather than being preceded by a period of worry and depression' – John Harvey-Jones

Much the same can be said about self-discipline.

We have all worked with very talented people who, though aware of their strengths, had real difficulty doing the next task that needs to be done today. Without an externally imposed deadline, ideally from someone in authority, they just cannot pick up and do even the simplest chore in front of them. Needless to say, this has a corrosive effect on their courage and reduces their capacity to generate opportunity.

Those who are naturally self-disciplined (like Karl) often have difficulty understanding this. They simply don't experience that level of paralysis; so they are tempted to treat it as lazy dysfunction. The challenge for Karl is recognising that sometimes a shift in focus is necessary, and this is not a sign of weakness or ill-discipline. Maria understands this, she knows that a shift in focus is required. While Karl rates himself higher than Maria, Maria may find this gateway easier to access.

This gateway is not an appealing one for people such as Graham who are easy-going and spontaneous. They will be tempted to dismiss self-discipline entirely. Or they may have an intellectual awareness that some level of self-discipline is beneficial, but may not have sufficient motivation or conviction to act upon it.

Self-discipline cannot be cultivated by reading about it. If someone is a hostage to their mood, it is usually helpful to start work on another gateway first, so as to build some energy. But self-discipline cannot be evaded; without it courage will neither be consistent nor sustainable. Sure, there is benefit in going with the flow (or feeling of creativity or inspiration); but the equal necessity of self-discipline is unfortunately often overlooked.

Self-discipline is a particularly useful gateway for those with the following personality characteristics:

1. **Openness dimension: Consistent (vs Curious)**: Discipline comes easily to those who are consistent because they prefer to implement in a methodical disciplined way and are attentive to detail. These intrinsic qualities come together in the form of a disciplined, consistent approach to life. Who fits this description?

Adam, Janique and Karl all show evidence of being consistent in their habits. Even if Adam has let his recent regime go, he should be able to access this gateway via his characteristic of consistency.

2. **Conscientiousness dimension: Efficient and Organised (vs Easy-going and Spontaneous)**: Self-discipline is a characteristic of those who are efficient and organised. They are usually good at

controlling distractions and maintaining focus. Self-care is implicit in this as this group are good at managing themselves as well as their work. Who might fit this description?

Everyone except Graham, who is the polar opposite with his drunken nights on the sofa, endless takeaways and financial mess.

3. Extroversion dimension: Solitary (vs Outgoing): Being internally referenced, solitary people often appear controlled and disciplined. Their ability to introspect and their high levels of impulse-control manifest outwardly as a disciplined approach to life. Who does this describe?

Adam can easily fit this description once he recaptures his more organised life. Graham on the other hand will need to access this gateway through introspection and reflection. If he can harness his natural curiosity to examine healthier options, he can go on to access this gateway. But he probably shouldn't start with self-discipline; it's too unattractive for him.

4. Agreeableness dimension: Challenging (vs Adaptable): The competitive, tough nature of the challenger often requires a rigid sense of discipline. Their desire to win at all costs and protect their interests means they naturally tend towards this gateway. This is the preserve of many a great sporting hero. Who fits this description?

Graham is a challenger who has lost his competitive edge. But he is a challenger nevertheless and if he can reignite his desire to win, this will give him energy and self-discipline will follow. Karl is also a challenger, and understandably he rates his self-discipline highly.

5. Neuroticism dimension: Assured (vs Sensitive): Those who don't vacillate between the emotional 'highs and lows' will find this gateway more accessible. They have the advantage of being more 'urge-resistant' and therefore focused. Who is focused in this way?

Maria is a good example of someone who is 'assured' and managing her emotions in the midst of a stressful career. Despite his lack of experience, Adam is not a hostage to emotional states and so has a natural advantage here. Karl is 'assured' almost to an extreme, and while this makes self-discipline accessible, it can also make it difficult to switch approach when the marketplace changes around him.

Top tips to help you become more Self-disciplined

1. Developing your muscle Self-discipline is like a muscle – the more you use it the better you get at it. But just like a muscle it is weak to start with and needs building up. Start with small things and work up. Some find it useful to begin with making small changes to their rising- or bedtimes, others start with their eating habits, still others begin by just clearing a corner of their desk. Start wherever is easiest for you.

2. Making phone calls For example, if you are currently making no sales calls in the average week, start by diarising one appointment in the next twenty-four hours rather than ten by the end of the week. Build on the success of making one call and others will follow. Diarising time to make regular calls builds habits of self-discipline.

3. Taming your task list While some are slaves to the task list, others have a cavalier attitude to the to-do list. Their list is a random list of good ideas, items carried forward and a host of things that they have no intention of doing today. It can be useful to put an unworkable list aside, and just note a top three that you *commit* to doing today. Everything else is a bonus. This tends to restore confidence, and within a few days enhances self-respect and capacity to act.

15

Sixth Gateway – Curiosity and Creativity

'Variety's the very spice of life /
That gives it all its flavour' – *William Cowper*

As we prepared this chapter, we (Kate and John) were struck by all the coaching sessions we have done over the years with professionals who were struggling to stay engaged, often with years of success behind them. In our sessions with them, we would often find ourselves saying something like: 'So, what you are telling me is that you're bored?' The sigh of relief accompanying this admission was often palpable.

It seems that boredom is one of the key afflictions of successful professionals. How is it that something that starts out as creative and exciting can easily become repetitive and boring?

Many people articulate other issues such as shortage of time, changing markets, leadership, financial pressure, conflict, succession, planning, etc. But dig just a little deeper and explore why talented people are not dealing with these issues, and sooner or later you will start hearing about the dreaded daily 'treadmill', the constant struggle with that boring task list that keeps them bogged down.

Curiosity and creativity are about change and restlessness. They're the desire to learn new things about yourself and the world and the tolerance and acceptance of the unknown. Curiosity is a readiness to explore and capitalise on opportunity.

So how do curiosity and creativity build courage? Curiosity opens up new options, new ideas and a willingness to explore new resources and perspectives. Out of this exploration, new options and new resources to act appear. This enhances our capacity to act, and gives us the means to cope with risk, fear and uncertainty.

This, of course, presupposes that we have the ability to choose between options, which is where self-discipline and the other gateways come into play (for example, Purpose and Meaning, Communication Skill, etc.).

People who are curious and creative like asking questions. They seek variety and novelty. They may get bored easily but they know how to shake things up and change the field of play. They use their internal restlessness to great effect, relying on this inner spirit and not the world around them to create change. Curiosity and creativity drive a spirit of enquiry that opens the gateway to courage.

But boredom can strike in any situation. Let's look at some common examples.

Filled with vision, an entrepreneur forms a company. Jumping all the hurdles of the first few years, the sales pipeline and the service delivery eventually gets established. As the business grows, new people are recruited, and there are new challenges in management. Change comes from external sources. So far, so good. When the entrepreneur has successfully established the business, they will have learned a lot about business development, management, developing people and a host of other experiences that you cannot have in business school. Then what?

A similar excitement accompanies early career. When Adam finds a job, hopefully it will be one that motivates him. As his experience grows, new doors will open and his ability to cultivate opportunity (once learned) will rapidly enhance his promotion prospects. He may well be in senior management within a few years, though he may find this hard to believe just now. When Adam arrives at that mountain peak, what will he strive for next? Another mountain peak? But sooner or later, won't all mountain peaks look like 'more of the same'? Once he has arrived at partnership or directorship or whatever constitutes a 'peak', or once he is financially independent… what will he do with the rest of his professional life?

For all too many talented people, life turns into more of the same. Change is no longer driven by external factors such as career advancement. We've already seen some of this with Maria, though in her case the problem has probably been compounded by other issues. There comes a point in every professional's life when change and challenging what's new have to come from within.

Imagine you are a dentist, with an established practice. You do your fifteen plus appointments every day, as you have been doing every day for the past twenty years. There is not a cavity you have not seen. As you look ahead at the years in front of you, you see at least another fifteen years of this... perhaps more if anything nasty happens to your investments. What is it like to come to work on a Monday morning?

Systems and procedures

There has always been a degree of routine in work. No matter how visionary the stonemason was about his cathedral (see Chapter 11), cutting stone every day is a routine task. Yet it often appears that routine-isation is gaining ground. A generation ago, a visit to your doctor was primarily an encounter between two human beings. Now there is more procedure to follow and, measured by the minute, the eyes of your GP are more likely to be on the computer screen than on you.

While words such as 'creativity' and 'innovation' are used freely, how much room is there really for this? Surely 'control' and 'deliverables' are much more in evidence. If a team member goes to the boss with a proposal to spend four hours per week building the firm's reputation in a new market, what will be uppermost in the boss's mind: creative innovation, or the loss of valuable hours?

In most organisations, control wins. It takes a very brave manager to remove the control; it seems that anyone can add another one.

Mental stimulation

The problem is compounded by the fact that professionals need an above-average degree of mental stimulation. Many professionals chose their careers because of the opportunity this afforded them to solve interesting problems. Whether this was the doctor healing patients, the tax adviser saving money or the HR specialist who wanted to develop a positive culture, their vision was making a difference by contributing solutions to complex problems.

Even when the vision is realised, a professional still needs space to develop and grow. There needs to be some room every week to 'sharpen the saw' as Stephen Covey put it. Cultivating new opportunity can be one way for a professional to take on some genuine 'new challenges'.

What happens if they don't? One of the inevitable casualties is that courage suffers. A professional may well 'get away with' routine for months or years, but this retreat leads to a shrinking comfort zone. When the day comes that courage is needed, perhaps to face major change or redundancy, the muscles of courage are flaccid and powerless.

Play and creativity

The need for novelty and variety does not stop at the office door. Janique's daily grind of *métro, boulot, dodo* (metro, work, sleep) also erodes courage and diminishes resilience. If the work is interesting, this helps, but even then professionals need to relax and unwind.

Many will acknowledge that work, rest and play are valuable dimensions of a balanced lifestyle. But are these ingredients really essential to courage? What is it about play and creativity that constitutes a gateway?

Play may be indeed optional for some, but mental stimulation is essential. So is rest, and this is covered more fully in the next gateway (Physical Stamina). If mental stimulation is absent, energy diminishes and so does courage. The boring treadmill may be secure; indeed that's precisely the problem. Over time, the professional loses the elasticity to change, adapt and learn. So, when an upheaval or reorganisation comes along, a rigid professional is ill-equipped to deal with it.

On the other hand, those who are constantly interested and learning have the advantage. Curiosity makes your mind active instead of passive. Curious people are always asking questions and searching for answers in their minds. Their minds are always on the go. Since the mind is like a muscle which becomes stronger through continual exercise, the mental exercise caused by curiosity makes the minds of curious people stronger and stronger. The muscles of their minds are exercised, and hence are supple and adaptable. It's better to anchor our security on a capacity to adapt and be curious (internally developed and exercised) rather than rely on a fixed routine (externally given). We are then in charge of our destiny, not just hostages to fortune.

Curiosity is the foundation of creativity. It makes your mind observant of new ideas. When you are curious about something, your mind expects and anticipates new ideas related to it. When the ideas come they will soon be recognised. Without curiosity, the ideas may pass right in front of you and yet you miss them because your mind is not prepared to recognise them. Hence the wisdom of that Eastern saying: 'When the student is ready, the teacher will appear.'

Creativity is an active rather than a passive state. This means being able to spot the value of an idea, and make the connection necessary to solve the problem. This puts those who can access this gateway at a great advantage in terms of spotting opportunity. Opportunities usually arise when connections are made: for example, a connection between a group's 'needs' and another group's 'resources'. Those who can make the connection are able to spot the opportunity.

By being curious you will be able to see new worlds and possibilities which are normally not visible. It takes a curious mind to look beneath the surface and discover these new worlds and possibilities.

The life of curious people is far from boring. It's neither dull nor routine. There are always new things that attract their attention and give them energy.

The ability to unlock your curiosity and creativity requires certain conditions. Not being too busy/scheduled is critical. You need time to let your mind wonder and ask questions. We have to be able to 'create space' if we want our ideas to have room to develop and flourish. We have to give ourselves room to challenge and be curious. Just plain old time off to relax is also valuable. When we run or listen to music or walk in the sunshine we allow our brains the option of using many more of its regions. We open ourselves up to the possibility of new connections and the right-hand side of the brain has a chance to work more effectively. We literally increase our brainpower. Paradoxically, by slowing ourselves down in this way we increase our capacity.

So where are you? Taking work and play together, to what extent are you stimulated and interested by your current daily life?

4 = High: lots of stimulation and challenge, in a positive environment

3 = Good: though constantly pulled back into routine, limited room for curiosity

2 = OK: but could be better. Dominated by routine. Insufficient opportunity for mental challenge.

1 or 0 = Trapped on a treadmill, lack of stimulation, creativity and curiosity

At this time, we are measuring current reality. Perhaps it was different a year ago, and/or you hope it will change in the future. Right now, we are looking at the *current* access to this gateway.

Adam:

'Low, I'm afraid. Right now, just a 1. I keep myself sane by learning C#, but I don't really know where this is going. Really need to get into some kind of solution construction, if only for my own sanity.'

Janique:

'Also low. Though for the last six months, I appreciated the fact that the job was easy, and didn't require my brain. I needed that. But now I'm feeling I have more capacity: 2.'

Maria:

'Although I have many questions about my job, I don't complain about a lack of mental stimulation. I certainly get pulled back into management stuff, but that is part of the job. I have team members caught up in the compliance-trap of HR, but I'm fortunate to be at a level above that.

'For me, the problem lies more with the meaning of it all. Here I need to get some perspective. But I do appreciate what I've got: this is a 4.'

Karl:

'Like Maria, I cannot say that I'm bored. Worried, yes… but bored, no. So I'm not so convinced this is an important issue for me. Let's say 3.'

Graham:
'To be honest, I'm dying of boredom. My law practice frequently feels like a millstone around my neck. I often dream of closing it and just going around the world on my own for a year. I don't believe my life has any creativity in it. So my score is a total zero, and I do acknowledge this is a very appealing gateway for me. Not too sure where to start, but certainly curious.'

Mental energy

Just as a sluggish body nourished on poor quality food will exhibit poor energy levels, much the same is true of the mind. If the only exercise it gets is 'jumping to conclusions' (Danny Kaye) then sooner or later the muscles get rigid and the elasticity needed to adapt is not there any more.

Absence of mental stimulation can cause other gateways to close. If Adam cannot exercise his talents, how long will he continue to believe in them, and what will happen to his strength-based self-awareness? And hence to his connection with others? To date, Janique has benefited from a job that didn't require her brain, but if that persisted for years, how might her communication skills be affected?

And as for Graham, who has a strong innate sense of curiosity, he is (perhaps literally) 'dying of boredom'. The daily grind of a law practice has nearly snuffed out the talented brilliance that Hannah so admired when she first came to work for him.

All of these gateways tend to influence each other. Courage will be more accessible via some than via others. Both brain and heart are important resources: nobody is obliged to choose between them. Curiosity and creativity nourish our brains. Variety adds spice to life.

This gateway is particularly useful for those with the following personality characteristics:

1. Openness to experience dimension: Curious (vs Consistent):
While discipline comes easily to those who are consistent, curiosity comes just as naturally to those who score highly on 'Openness to experience'. We have already seen that Graham is 'dying of boredom'; who else is naturally curious and could really use this gateway?

Maria would also score highly on Curiosity, and so can also find courage through this gateway.

2. Conscientiousness dimension: Easy-going and Spontaneous (vs Efficient and Organised): Being less attached to specific outcomes and plans than others, those who are spontaneous can also find this gateway very accessible. When they feel free to try new things, this enhances their courage. When they feel trapped, they feel discouraged. Who fits this description?

Graham: all the others score higher than Graham on 'Conscientiousness'.

3. Extroversion dimension: All: In practice, both Solitary and Outgoing people can access this gateway. Solitary intellectual people, who have an insatiable appetite for learning, can feed their courage in this way. More extroverted people are likely to exercise their curiosity with others.

4. Agreeableness dimension: All: Again, this gateway is open to both Adaptable and Challenging people. Those who possess a challenging mindset can make use of curiosity to enlarge their world. If not, scepticism can create a shrinking world and a descent into bitterness. Who could enlarge his world in this way?

Both Karl and Graham. Karl could use a bit of play and creativity to relieve his frustration, which could turn sour. If Graham could rekindle a passion or interest in something outside work that would in turn give him renewed courage in his professional life, and stop the potential slide into depression that may have already begun.

5. Neuroticism dimension: All: Both Sensitive and Assured people can use this gateway. Those who are Sensitive will come up with ideas to which they will often feel emotionally connected, and that may cloud the quality of their judgement. Assured types are more likely to appraise ideas more neutrally and become less entrenched.

Top tips to help you develop Curiosity and Creativity

1. Deciding to be creative The main thing that hinders creative thinking is our belief that we are not creative. If you tell yourself 'I am a creative person', then you have to have beliefs about yourself that support that identity. If you tell yourself 'I am just an ordinary human being', then you will have a different set of beliefs. Once you have a particular identity and set of beliefs about yourself, you will become interested in seeking out the skills needed to express your identity and beliefs. If you believe that you are 'uncreative', then there is no need to learn how to become creative.

2. Keeping an open mind This is essential if you are to have a curious mind. Be open to learn, unlearn, and relearn. Some things you know and believe in might be wrong, and you should be prepared to accept this possibility and change your mind.

3. Asking questions relentlessly A sure way to dig deeper beneath the surface is asking questions: What is that? Why is it made that way? When was it made? Who invented it? Where does it come from? How does it work? What, why, when, who, where, and how are the best friends of curious people.

4. Don't label something as boring Whenever you label something as boring, you close one more door of possibilities. Curious people are unlikely to call something boring. Instead, they always see it as a door to a new world. Even if they don't yet have time to explore it, they will leave the door open to be visited another time.

5. Reading diverse kinds of literature Don't spend too much time on just one world; take a look at another world. It will introduce you to the possibilities and excitement of the other worlds which may spark your interest to explore them further. One easy way to do this is through reading diverse kinds of literature. Try to pick a book or magazine on a new subject and let it feed your mind with the excitement of a new world.

6. Doing one thing differently every day Take a different route to work. Buy different brands of butter. Swap desks with someone at work and get a different perspective on the office. Whatever little thing it is, do it – it all adds up and keeps you receptive and open to opportunity.

16

Seventh Gateway – Physical Stamina

> *'We must no more ask whether the soul and*
> *body are one than ask whether the wax and the*
> *figure impressed on it are one' – Aristotle*

In contrast to those previous generations who performed physical work, most of us now spend our time just sitting around. Our occupations are sedentary and the opportunity for physical movement is frequently restricted. A walk to the coffee machine, a visit to the bathroom and to the kitchen to make a coffee may well be the total sum of a morning's physical activity.

By contrast, our minds are whirring at top speed. The synapses of our brains are processing, anticipating, analysing, assessing, reading, absorbing, typing... the list goes on. The contrast between our physical inertia and our mental hurriedness is striking. Hunched over a keyboard, 8 per cent of our body-mass is a hive of activity, while 92 per cent is just sitting in a chair all day.

Yet mental activity is tiring, too. A day of stressful meetings or tasks can leave us feeling tired and lethargic and unwilling to contemplate exercise. When evening comes, we just want to flop down into a chair with a glass of wine and not engage in physical activity.

But this is a dangerous cycle. The mind and body are inextricably linked. The mind can't function unless the body is working properly – and it also works the other way around. The state of our minds affects our bodies. If we feel low, tired or anxious, we may do less and become less active – which can make us feel worse and we can easily get caught in a harmful cycle.

As a result, it's hardly surprising that the physical dimension of one's life often becomes invisible. Snack bars are hastily substituted for food that takes too much time to prepare. The necessity of visiting the bathroom is resented as an unwelcome interruption to a busy schedule. We 'forget' to go to the gym. The necessities of the mental dimension dominate the needs of physical health.

Physical stamina is the ability to perform intense work over a prolonged period of time. People with high physical stamina seem to have enduring energy, strength and resilience. Physical exercise increases our stamina, which seems to protect us and allow us to achieve more rather than less. In thinking about why this should be, it's worth noting an evolutionary perspective. Most people in the world have always had to keep active to get food, water and shelter. This involves a moderate level of activity and seems to make us feel good. Research from the Royal College of Psychiatrists suggests we may be built – or 'hard wired' – to enjoy a certain amount of exercise. We need exercise and physical stamina to thrive.

Exercise also seems to have an effect on certain chemicals in the brain, like dopamine and serotonin. Brain cells use these chemicals to communicate with each other, so they affect your mood and thinking. Exercise can stimulate other chemicals in the brain called 'brain derived neurotrophic factors'. These help new brain cells to grow and develop, allowing us to do more, think better, etc.

Exercise also seems to reduce harmful changes in the brain caused by stress. With stress levels reaching epidemic proportions even in young children, physical activity seems to provide welcome protection. A chink of light for those who hate exercise: moderate exercise seems to work better than the vigorous kind.

It is not the purpose of this book to describe a healthy regime of diet and exercise. There are thousands of books on those topics, and most of us know far more about the subject than we are actually doing. Nowhere is the 'knowing–doing' gap so much in evidence. Understanding brain chemistry and the link between physical activity and mental activity can help us to understand how physical stamina enables us to access courage and hence cultivate opportunity.

The energy to cultivate opportunity

Physical stamina helps access courage by increasing our physical capacity to act. The release of positive brain chemicals as a by-product of physical activity helps our mood and predisposition to action. They also increase the level of connectivity in the brain, which helps both with learning and creativity.

The 'courage to ask' implies the energy to do so. Without a focus on stamina, that energy is often not there. While everyone benefits from good health, there are specific reasons why physical stamina is particularly important for those who need to cultivate opportunity.

First, there is a lot of work to do. Developing a business or finding a job is rarely a nine to five occupation. There is research, travel, lunches, social media, networking events, emails, follow-up tasks, proposals and breakfast meetings. If you are looking for an easy life, look elsewhere!

Second, there are ups and downs to deal with. No doubt everyone gets their share of these, but the share in opportunity creation is particularly generous. Meetings get cancelled at the last minute. Proposals and offers get rejected. There is lots of disappointment to contend with. People will refuse some of your requests, or not return your calls. If you are feeling physically tired, it's very easy to become demotivated by these setbacks and turn to energy-sapping props such as food, sugar or alcohol for comfort.

Third, the life of an opportunity cultivator is full of physical health hazards. All those lunches and cocktails don't make it easy to stay in shape. You may be staying in hotels away from home, and tempted by fabulous menus and cheese selections. The client may invite you to a boozy evening, of the very kind you are trying to resist. It can be hard to say No.

For many business people, the struggle with results is not just a struggle with strategy, but also a struggle with behaviour. It's often more tempting (and quicker) to change the strategy than to confront the behaviour change needed for success.

For example, a trainer might get on really well with people, be very articulate, and do plenty of networking. As a result, they get lots of business cards, from people who genuinely wish to stay in touch. But the trainer comes home from these events exhausted, and just hasn't got the energy to put these cards into a system for follow-up. After a few months of this, they naturally start to think that the networking 'just isn't working'.

But perhaps it is. Maybe it's the follow-up that needs attention. Even if the trainer knows this, they may lack the energy to do it. Being a bit unsure about how to proceed, the business cards sit in a drawer or a briefcase. After a few days, or weeks, any follow-up now seems inappropriate.

These people are already feeling guilty about not getting to the gym, or going out for a run, and that adds to their sense of fatigue. They already know what they should be doing, and if they could only bridge that 'knowing–doing gap', their capacity to act would be so much greater.

This is where courage comes in. We have already discussed this in the context of self-discipline (see Chapter 14). It takes self-discipline to do what we don't want to do. In this gateway, we are primarily focusing on energy, which is the fuel for the engine of self-discipline.

So what about your energy levels? Would you say that these are…

4 = Very high: feeling physically fit, energetic and ready for the task in hand

3 = Generally good: with moments of fatigue, occasionally forgetting to exercise or eat well

2 = Fair: I'm well aware that it could be better, and I'm frequently tired or sluggish

1 or 0 = Low: I just don't have the energy to do the things I know I could/should do

Adam:
'I know I have no excuse, being young and unemployed and all that, but I'm hesitating between a 1 and a 2. I've got no health problems, but I've totally lost interest in the sports that I used to do. Just don't seem to be able to get myself moving, particularly in the morning.'

Janique:
'Very low, zero. By the time I have worked, collected the children, come home, prepared food, put the children to bed, and applied for jobs, I am totally, totally, exhausted.'

Maria:

'Generally good, probably a 3. I have learned to deal with travel and hotels. I use the stairs rather than the lift: that has become my gym. I eat well, and if I could recover a sense of passion for my work I'm sure it would be a 4 again soon.'

Karl:

'My energy is good. I work off my worries in the gym, by running or weight-training. I'm physically fit, I eat well and I look after myself. Always have. It's a 4.'

Graham:

'Well, this is embarrassing. I take no exercise and my physical self-care is non-existent. Recently, there has also been a tendency to uncork too many wine bottles in the evening. The problem is that I don't feel motivated to do anything about this right now. Never been much of a sporting lad, really. The prospect of vigorous exercise does not really appeal. So... a zero?'

Attitude

With the exception of Janique, it's interesting how the energy habits of four people have *little* to do with their current situation and everything to do with their attitude. Even for Janique, whose situation is the most hamstrung of the five, her attitude is influencing her relationship with exercise (she believes it has to be formal, she does not see she can build stamina in day-to-day life, as Maria sees). Karl is worried and working hard, yet still finds time for formal exercise and he eats well. Furthermore, it appears he always has done so. Despite constant travel and a loss of passion in her work, Maria still manages to maintain a healthy lifestyle, too. On the other hand, Adam feels sluggish despite lots of time on his hands, and Graham just cannot bring himself to care.

Some people succeed in kick-starting their 'courage turnaround' from this gateway. For them, the 'courage to ask' begins with physical movement, for example, exercise – rather than mental rearrangement such as a new set of career tactics or a new marketing strategy. By rising earlier in the morning and going for a run – and prioritising this above all else – one can sometimes find the energy to deal with a pile of business cards.

Janique's perception of her situation makes this gateway difficult to access right now. In reality, she could do a workout from a DVD at home. Or play Wii Fit. It is her attitude that holds her back, not her circumstances.

Beyond 'sophisticated procrastination', there is always something we can do even if that involves shifting our perspective; for example, Janique can climb stairs just as Maria does. Whatever about his circumstances, Graham clearly finds this gateway inaccessible, though he is equating stamina with 'vigorous exercise' which does not have to be the case. If Graham went for a twenty-minute walk each day he would see improvements in his productivity and mental well-being because his brain would be firing and connecting better and the neurochemicals associated with well-being would increase. For Adam, a thirty-minute workout may kick-start a build-up of courage, that will in turn open doors to fresh opportunity and well-being at the same time.

While this gateway is open to all, it is apparent that not everyone sees it that way. It's particularly accessible for those with the following personality characteristics:

1. Openness dimension: Consistent (vs Curious): Most routine comes easily to those who are consistent, so a healthy routine can easily form a permanent part of those professionals' experiences, in turn creating courage and energy. Who could benefit immediately?
Adam: he has both the time and the 'consistency' to keep it up.

2. Conscientiousness dimension: All: Structuring time for exercise will come easily to those of our friends who are efficient and organised. Their intent to exercise is high, but whether they will execute on that intent is another story. Nevertheless, easy-going people can also access this gateway if they keep it pleasurable. It is likely to be less structured and more opportunistic. Conscientiousness only impacts attitude or intent to exercise, it does not impact actual exercise behaviour.

3. Extroversion dimension: Outgoing (vs Solitary): In fairness, both Solitary and Outgoing people can access this gateway. However it seems to be particularly accessible to outgoing people who can make friends and have fun at the same time. Golf is a classic example of a social activity that also builds stamina.

4. Agreeableness dimension: Challenging (vs Adaptable): People who are challengers have a preference for concrete achievement and they do things that they perceive to be in their own interests. They also have that need to win, the competitive edge and endurance that often drives them to succeed in sport. Who springs to mind?

Karl is the obvious example of this: it's no surprise that he works out regularly. Graham is also a challenger, but he lacks the consistency, efficiency and organisation of Karl.

5. Neuroticism dimension: Assured (vs Sensitive): People who are assured and hardy tend to be relaxed under pressure. We learned earlier that physical exercise actively reduces the harmful effects of stress so these types are getting a double benefit by accessing courage in this way. Highly sensitive types have a more negative attitude to exercise, and are more prone to feeling embarrassed and self-conscious about it. Who might fit this description?

Janique and Graham. Janique blames her situation and Graham avoids exercise entirely. If they were to start, they would probably feel self-conscious about exercise at first. This is where self-awareness (fourth gateway) can help, anticipating and overcoming initial resistance.

Rest

With all this frenetic mental activity, it's hardly surprising that many people have trouble switching off. According to a survey carried out by the UK's Mental Health Foundation in 2011, nearly two-thirds of respondents reported some sleep problems. We (the authors) see the same theme cropping up in our coaching work with individual clients: the inability to rest is now a recurring problem in professional life.

Many people find one of the extra benefits of physical exercise is better sleep. Others find the key to success is avoiding stressful tasks (or TV programmes!) in the hours immediately before going to bed. The problems of rest constitute a very large and complicated area, about which an entire book could probably be written.

Fatigue does not simply result from a heavy workload. If the stonemason in Chapter 11 was happy in his life and his work, he probably slept well. David Whyte puts it well: 'The antidote to exhaustion is not necessarily rest; the antidote to exhaustion is wholeheartedness.' When there is purpose and meaning in what we do, when we trust our strengths and our capacity to deal with life's surprises, when we feel a sense of connection with others who care about us, we can rest in the knowledge that we will have the courage to try again tomorrow.

'A field that is rested gives a beautiful crop' – Ovid

Top tips to help with physical stamina

1. Taking simple steps You do not have to train for a marathon to access this gateway. Build in simple self-care routines that allow you to build your stamina. Get off the bus a stop early, switch escalators or lifts for stairs, switch one journey a week to walking or cycling – you don't need to do these things every single day, but increase the frequency with which you do them.

2. Massage, meditation and yoga are all good ways to build up fitness.

3. Walking and talking Walk your meetings. There is a whole new movement of having meetings on the move (started by a psychotherapist in Central Park). It fires the brain in a different way, can help with power dynamics and facilitates quieter people to speak. There are many benefits to a meeting on the physical move.

4. Recording what you actually do Many people 'aspire' to exercise – join gyms, tell others about their plans and then never quite make the gym class or the run they told their colleagues they were going on. Be aware of the difference between your intent and your actual behaviour – especially if you are high on Conscientiousness. Use a diary to keep a record of what you actually do.

5. Choosing carefully The activity you decide to incorporate in your life should be enjoyable – if you don't know what you might enjoy, try a few different things. It should help you to feel more competent, or capable. Gardening or DIY projects can do this, but don't try and do something that you feel you will be lousy at or that will give you a sense of failure. Ideally the activity will give you a sense of control over your life – that you have choices you can make (so it isn't helpful if you start to feel that you *have* to exercise). The sense that you are looking after yourself can also feel good.

6. Trying finding an exercise or activity buddy The companionship involved can be just as important as the physical activity, particularly for extroverts and agreeable people.

Part three

17
Adam Starts Asking

'A journey of a thousand miles begins with a single step'
– Lao Tzu

Adam came away from these exercises with mixed feelings. Reflecting back on his sporting achievements at school, his popularity at university and his talent for technology, he first felt ashamed at how he was letting himself go. Images of a pot-bellied, forty-something, unemployed geek began to haunt his imagination.

On the other hand, he felt encouraged by the thought that he could find courage (and opportunity) via his *own* choice of gateways. It had often occurred to Adam that extroverts like Joe and Emily seemed to have an unfair advantage. Extroverts made good first impressions, they did well in interviews, they found it easy to start a conversation with strangers. Most self-help books seemed to be written by extroverts, advocating extrovert practices that solitary people found hard to implement. A multiple-gateway approach was different, and encouraging.

Adam was also struck by the realisation that he was not 'asking'. Indeed, the more he thought about it, 'asking' had not been a part of his upbringing. As a child, he seemed to have learned that it was impolite to ask. As he walked to the station, he realised that he was going to have to unlearn some of this, and make a lot more requests than would feel comfortable. And that's where courage would be important. Right. Got it.

Strong start

On the train home, Adam re-scored each gateway, based not just on how he felt, but the accessibility of each gateway based on his personality characteristics. These came up as follows:

His OCEAN Characteristics: Consistent, Efficient and Organised, Solitary, Adaptable, Assured

GATEWAY	Initial Score (How he felt)	Accessibility Score	Based on Characteristics of... (See Chapter 9)
Connection to others	3	1	Adaptable
Purpose and Meaning	1	3	Consistent, Efficient, Solitary
Influence and Communication Skill	1	4	Consistent, Efficient, Adaptable, Assured
Self-awareness	3	4	Efficient, Solitary, Adaptable, Assured
Self-discipline	1	4	Consistent, Efficient, Solitary, Assured
Curiosity and Creativity	1	3	Solitary, Adaptable, Assured
Physical Stamina	1	3	Consistent, Efficient, Assured

Adam's first conclusion was that there were more gateways open to him than he had ever imagined. He decided to start with some Self-discipline, on the basis that it would come fairly easily to him. Self-discipline was within his control to work on and it would raise his energy level for the other gateways.

His parents were a little surprised when he announced he was going to bed early, as he planned to rise at 7 am and go for a run. They were even more surprised when he started doing this every morning, no matter what the weather. Sensing that something positive was afoot, they didn't say too much, remembering that Adam could be very disciplined and consistent when he wanted to.

Adam's knowledge of sports training was sufficient for him to know that it's important to take it easy at first, in order to avoid injury. He downloaded a fairly gentle regime from the Internet, and avoided the temptation to do too much at once. He also decided to make this a metaphor for the other gateways: to stretch himself gently but consistently, rather than going too far too fast and just pulling a muscle.

Influence and Communication Skill

Even before the benefits of running became evident, Adam felt good that he was starting something new, a project he was creating himself rather than following some preordained 'seven steps to heaven' approach. Looking at the other gateways that came up for him, in particular Influence and Communication Skill, Adam decided it was time to have a chat with Joe.

Adam wanted to explain what he was doing, and he also wanted to tell Joe why he couldn't really go on that ski holiday. If he was ever going to practise the courage to ask, he felt he would have to start with someone he knew well. Adam was still none too sure what he was asking for, so he settled for asking Joe for ideas.

Joe was not only supportive with ideas; he passed on to Adam a free day pass that he had been gifted for a local health club. Adam visited the club, and was impressed by the facilities, the pool, the tennis courts... perhaps even the possibility of meeting other friendly people there.

So Adam embarked on another 'ask'. Sitting down with his parents, he explained what he was doing and asked them to buy his membership to the club for six months. They agreed readily enough. Even if they found it hard to see the connection between going to the gym and getting a job, they kept that observation to themselves. Sensing a renewed determination in Adam's eyes, they wanted to do all they could to support and encourage him.

Having made a start with Self-discipline, done something with Influence and Communication Skill and indeed Physical Stamina, Adam felt good that he was making progress. As he visited the club each day, he was becoming more and more aware of his power to act and he was enjoying himself in the process. Soon he found himself looking at the other gateways and wondering what to do next. His daily visit to the health club was certainly a source of variety, and soon Adam began to recognise faces in the spinning classes and in the gym. But it was not mentally challenging, and Adam began to wonder what he could do to workout his mental muscles as much as his physical ones. And of course, he was still looking for job openings.

Above all, Adam recognised he needed to do more with Influence and Communication Skill, but for that he needed more interaction with people. In this domain, he just didn't know where to start. He also realised he was a bit isolated. While he was happy enough on his own, continuing his study of C# and going to the sports club, he didn't exactly have any friends there. He would nod and smile at people in the spinning class, but they always seemed to be in such a hurry.

When reflecting on 'asking', it occurred to Adam that he could create his own little research project in order to find out which technical skills would be most in demand for the future. At least, this would be an excuse to start reconnecting with some people. And it would help to get him into the habit of asking; a habit that Adam now realised he needed to cultivate. It would also be a tangible opportunity to practise Influence and Communication Skills.

As he didn't want to come across as desperate, Adam decided to prepare these calls well. He realised he would have to explain what he was doing, and the easiest way to explain it was with the simple truth: he wanted to know which skills he should next learn. It would be a simple request, a reasonable one, and a good way to get a call started. He also created a profile on LinkedIn, and thought about converting his Facebook contacts into LinkedIn contacts, so that he might explore the professional networks to which they belonged.

At about this time, Adam hit his first big roadblock. He'd been told there would be roadblocks and that courage would be needed in order to resist the temptations of sophisticated procrastination. He knew that ideally these conversations should take the form of phone calls or face-to-face meetings, but he was sorely tempted to make the connection by email. Yet Adam knew that while an email exchange might give him the information he was after, it would not really build (or rebuild) the connection (and the interaction) in the way that he wanted. Yet he resisted making those calls.

Adam recognised the phenomenon of 'sophisticated procrastination'. He felt more tempted to build a system than to get on with the calls. The more he thought about it, the harder it got. Though he knew he was doing so (Self-awareness), Adam still shirked the fence.

Blocked by what?

Adam looked again at the gateways, searching for the courage to make contact. What was he missing? After all, these were not strangers; many of them were people that he used to know well. He had a reasonable question to ask them. What was holding him back?

Somehow, Adam did not feel *entitled* to make the call. Even though he had a reasonable request, he might be interrupting the people he was calling at a difficult moment. They were busy people, and would they think: 'I wonder what Adam is really after. If he wants a job, why doesn't he just come right out and say it?'

Once again, Adam knew that sophisticated procrastination was at work, and he consoled himself with the thought that he was at least clearing some of the overgrowth around the fourth gateway of Self-awareness. Rationally, he knew that if the moment of the call was not right, he could just arrange a better time. Ultimately, he knew that other people's opinion of him was none of his business, anyway.

But he still didn't want to make the call.

'Focus on strengths,' they said. Perhaps he could just arrange a party, and call the people he knew? The problem with that was that many of them now lived far away, and anyway some of the people he wanted to talk to were not people he knew well enough, so they would find it very strange if they suddenly got a call out of the blue inviting them to a party. Mmmm. Blocked again.

Entitlement

There was a gateway left unexplored: the second, Purpose and Meaning. In theory, it was also a gateway that came up as very accessible for him, though for the life of him, he could not see how. Adam acknowledged that he was a bit wary about this gateway, and couldn't understand why it should score '3' for him, based on personality characteristics of Consistent, Efficient and Organised, and Solitary. He didn't have any grand purposes or visions. If anything, he was a bit wary of people who did.

In any case, no matter what his purpose turned out to be, wouldn't he always run up against this issue of *entitlement*? As for Influence and Communication Skill, well that's the space he wanted to get to, but perhaps he really lacked the courage to get there?

Drawing on his Self-awareness, Adam took a sheet of paper and resolved to honestly analyse himself. What was the root issue? As he dug deeper, he realised that the crucial issue was this problem of *entitlement*. He had once heard somebody say that each of us is entitled to call anyone in the world. The other person is certainly entitled to refuse the call, but we are entitled to make it. The problem for Adam is that he just didn't *feel* entitled. His brain might accept that he was entitled, but his stomach didn't believe his brain and his hand certainly did not want to pick up that phone.

One possible solution would be for Adam to send a message asking when he could speak to the other person, and it did occur to him that this would be easier. Perhaps the other person would not reply. If so, would he try a second time?

Adam realised he was still stuck on this issue of entitlement, the medium of the message was not the problem. His entitlement to send it was the issue. Where could that entitlement come from? Somehow, it would have to be derived from the *purpose* of his call, the *reason* he was getting in touch.

Adam and Janique had kept in touch, and in one late-night Skype, Adam shared with Janique how he could not build a sufficient sense of entitlement to make the call.

'So what?' Janique replied. She reminded Adam that courage is not the absence of fear, rather the decision that something else was more important than the fear. For Janique, this was her children. What was it for Adam? What was going to make the task worthwhile?

Suddenly, Adam saw the significance of the second gateway (Purpose and Meaning). He realised he had been looking for entitlement as a prerequisite to his actions, when in fact entitlement would come later, as a result of his actions. What he really needed was a compelling *reason* to accept the fear and do the call anyway. What was this reason? What was his purpose in getting a job?

'Do you know, Janique, I never really thought about that. It's just the next thing you do, right? After college. Finding your corner of the marketplace, earning money, achieving something. For what?… I don't know!'

People and technology

So what would make all this effort worthwhile for Adam? What would be a sufficient reason to overcome the lack of entitlement and make the call anyway?

The more Adam reflected on this, the more he realised that deep down he didn't want to be a backroom software developer. He might not be a raging extrovert but nevertheless, he enjoyed a certain amount of interaction with people. He wanted a career where he could collaborate and solve problems with other professionals. Adam felt at home both with people and technology, and his best moments at university were those when a good team contributed to solve problems together. Just for now, that was perhaps sufficient purpose for him: to be part of a team that solved complex problems through collective effort.

So, where are the best opportunities to combine people interaction with software development? Now here was a question that Adam could go and ask; a question that somehow pushed the issue of entitlement to one side. There was a reason to make the call.

From this point onwards, Adam's story accelerates. It did not take many conversations for Adam to discover that mobile-app development is a perfect environment for someone who has the talent of interacting with people as well as technical skill: more so than the engineering applications of C#. Adam's mornings quickly changed direction, though he kept up his health-club activities in the afternoon.

One afternoon, a tutorial manual fell out of his sports bag and triggered a conversation with the guy who picked it up and handed it back to Adam in the locker room. The two guys ended up having a coffee on the way out. A few days later, an informal chat followed in the same health-club café and Adam found himself being offered a job, without even a formal interview, and only a casual glance at that CV that he had spent hours perfecting only a few months before.

When Adam now looks back, he smiles at how accessible all of the gateways have become… from inside the castle, of course. There are still moments when he wonders where he will find the courage for that next conversation: the deadline that cannot be met, the team player who is not performing, or the awkward client that keeps changing scope. His employers were quick to spot his collaborative talent, and his responsibilities are evolving by the month.

Whatever the situation, Adam has disciplined himself to 'ask'. As he practices each 'ask', most conversations get easier.

COURAGEOUS QUESTIONS FOR JOBSEEKERS TO ASK:
- If I wanted to get good career advice, whom would I approach?
- What's driving growth in your company?
- In what areas will you be recruiting in the future?
- Where are you seeing the highest turnover of staff? Why?
- Who do you know who…?
- What's the salary/remuneration for…
- Which recruitment fairs are worth attending?
- Who does recruitment in your company? Would you be willing to introduce us? (Request)

COURAGEOUS REQUESTS FOR JOBSEEKERS TO MAKE:
- Would you be willing to review my CV?
- I would value a meeting with John, would you introduce us by email?
- May I ask you for an honest debrief… i.e. why did I not get that job?

- Would you be willing to take part in some research I am doing?
- May I call you again in three months to see how this is evolving?
- May I come and show you a prototype?

18

Les portes s'ouvrent

> *'There are no failures, just experiences and*
> *your reactions to them'* – Tom Krause

Janique was surprised to discover that she still had significant reserves of courage from which to draw. Until now, her experiences over the past five years had felt like a story of failure. Now, however, she began to uncover a strong sense of her own strength.

Like Adam, she reviewed both her initial scores, and the accessibility of each gateway based on her personality characteristics:

Her OCEAN Characteristics: Consistent, Efficient and Organised, Outgoing, Adaptable, Sensitive

GATEWAY	Initial Score (How she felt)	Accessibility Score	Based on Characteristics of... (see Chapter 9)
Connection to others	1	3	Outgoing, Adaptable, Sensitive
Purpose and Meaning	3	3	Consistent, Efficient, Sensitive
Influence and Communication Skill	1	4	Consistent, Efficient, Outgoing, Adaptable

Self-awareness	2	4	Efficient, Outgoing, Adaptable, Sensitive
Self-discipline	4	2	Consistent, Efficient
Curiosity and Creativity	2	3	Outgoing, Adaptable, Sensitive
Physical Stamina	0	3	Consistent, Efficient, Outgoing

Janique realised that she had been leaning heavily on Purpose and Meaning coupled with a relentless Self-discipline imposed more by necessity than by her personality. Nevertheless, she had survived most people's nightmare. She had succeeded in creating a happy home for her children after a divorce. She had not ended up being treated for depression, like her ex-husband. Without the capacity to act from a sense of purpose and meaning, she feared she might have gone under.

At the same time, she realised there were more gateways open to her than she was using to date. As she looked at the scores for Connection to Others and Influence and Communication Skill, she became painfully aware of her isolation. More than ever, the absence of peers and colleagues started to hurt, particularly when she remembered that she was partially responsible for this state of affairs.

Feeling ashamed of her loss of social status, she had avoided contact with people who had known her as a successful manager. When 'friend requests' had come via social media, for example, from university friends, she had not responded. She had deleted her old email account, and set up a new one for job search. She had changed her mobile number in order to avoid certain gossipy associates who had known both her and her husband. She had avoided neighbourhood gatherings, as she didn't want to belong where she now lived.

Janique acknowledged that she had played a part in constructing her current isolation. On the one hand, it had been a protective tactic. At the same time, the shell had turned into a wall. And behind the wall, Janique was hurting.

She started to remember how much she had enjoyed socialising in her early life. Both at university and later as a marketing manager, she thrived in the company of others. Yet the thought of reconnecting with former colleagues and friends did not exactly fill her with glee. Why?

Deep down, Janique felt that she had failed. Her career had failed, her marriage had failed, everything seemed to be broken. Except for her love for her children, a single bright spot in an otherwise bleak life.

So which gateways would help her overcome that sense of failure and enable her to reconnect with others? Looking at her scores, Self-awareness stood out, particularly the focus on strengths. What were the specific strengths that had enabled her to survive, when her ex-husband had gone under? Her strong sense of purpose, a capacity to make decisions and act upon them, the self-discipline and persistence to withstand a tough daily routine, her self-organisation. She had a talent for confronting reality and dealing with life on life's terms. Above all, she was adaptable.

The more Janique reflected on her strengths, the more she realised the need to redefine both success and failure. That old concept of success being linked to social status seemed almost medieval when compared to her ability to adapt to a twenty-first-century world. If success were the ability to adapt and to thrive, then she had proven that. She had discovered an inner strength that would be a resource in all conditions; whether other people recognised this or not.

Communicating

Janique realised that some courageous phone calls would be needed if she were to find her way out of the current impasse. Naturally, the first question was: Who?

And the second question was: When? Her present boss, though kind, was unlikely to tolerate personal calls at work, particularly if he became aware that these were directed towards finding another job. Evenings were full with children and preparation of food. In any case, Janique felt diffident about making some of these calls late in the evening. Furthermore, she did not always have mobile or home numbers for the people with whom she wanted to connect.

At this point, Janique recognised that sophisticated procrastination could be setting in. There certainly were some real issues to deal with; indeed that's what made the procrastination sophisticated. While listening to Adam's procrastination, Janique had recognised her own. So what was she going to do about it?

She decided to try out one phone call. She had been avoiding her former friend Giselle ever since that painful remark Giselle had made just before her divorce. When Janique changed her mobile number and email address, it was partly to cut Giselle off as much as it was to avoid others. The more she thought about it now, the more she felt ashamed of her own resentment. On more than a few occasions she had looked at Giselle's number, but each time that phone call seemed harder and harder to make.

In talking to Adam about how courage was not the absence of fear, but rather the decision that something else was more important, Janique recognised that the digits of Giselle's mobile number represented a unique and personal 'courage opportunity' for her. Trying to put her feelings of fear to one side, she dialled the digits one morning, but quickly hung up when she heard Giselle's voicemail message. However, during the afternoon, Janique realised she had broken the ice, so she decided to redial on the way home. When Giselle answered, Janique simply said 'Giselle, I'm calling to make amends... and to tell you a story.' The rest was easy.

It didn't always go so well. Some people were cool and distant, and Janique had to accept that her loss of status meant that some did not want to stay in touch. She decided that this was their problem, not hers. So be it. 'You are not responsible for how you are heard': this refrain rang in her ears. She would just focus on a few good friends, the rest she could afford to let go. She had lived without all of them and survived.

Making contact

In the days that followed, Janique got in touch with two more old friends and three former colleagues, one of whom had a very similar story to tell. It seemed that all over France, many *universitaires* were falling on tough times. Discovering she was not alone, Janique felt encouraged. All her friends promised support. Her former boss, Roland, suggested connecting on LinkedIn. 'Just go through all my connections, and tell me who you want to meet,' he said. 'I'll make it happen.'

Of course, it was rarely that simple. There were no vacancies in some organisations and there were some real gaps in Janique's experience, particularly around social media, which had evolved a lot since her days in marketing. The focus of her evenings began to change: less scrutinising of job sites, more study around current developments and tools. There was less broadcasting and more asking: asking for introductions, asking for advice on what to study, asking for feedback on a new CV that reflected some of those new skills Janique was now busy acquiring.

Janique asked her current boss for a slightly longer lunch break. In return, she offered to take some work home and do an evening turnaround with some of his requests. They agreed to review this weekly, and Janique had the courage to make this review really happen so that no resentment could accumulate. This new arrangement worked so well, the lunch breaks got longer and still her boss was happy with the new turnaround of work.

Janique was able to use this time to connect with former colleagues and ask for introductions. She remembered a tip about making an extra call every day, and applied that as diligently as her time allowed. Indeed, she often smiled when she thought of how well she used forty-five minutes now; often managing three conversations at lunchtime where in her previous marketing job this would have taken half a day.

The 'asks' began to accumulate, and soon the first interview was in the diary. This created a minor panic for Janique: the interview would necessitate time off work plus some new clothes. In the end, she asked Giselle for a small loan, though she found this really embarrassing and difficult to do. Then, just as she had spent the money and arranged the time off work, the interview was cancelled the day before it was due to happen. Janique was devastated.

Worse off

This was Janique's nadir: the lowest point of all. She started to wonder if all this talk of courage and resilience was not just building false expectations. Why not just accept life in a HLM, do her best for her kids, and end this struggle trying to find a job that perhaps would not even work out when she got there? If they cancelled interviews and changed their minds like this, how could she depend on companies like this, anyway?

To cope, she revisited her sense of purpose (second gateway) and particularly the opportunities she wanted to create for her children. Her objectives were not just her own; her purpose also had meaning. She reflected on the achievements of the previous six weeks, and the strength and self-awareness that were building up (fourth gateway). She felt good that she had connected with her friends again (first gateway), particularly when she remembered the courage it took to take these initiatives.

Despite the bitter disappointment of the cancelled interview, Janique felt she was 'on the way up'. The warmth and generosity of Giselle and other friends sustained her and she felt stronger than ever. Learning about social media was interesting (sixth gateway). She was certainly sleeping better than she had been for months (seventh gateway).

So what more could she do? Janique had been intrigued that physical stamina had come so high up on her list, so she decided to tone up her body via a gentle routine of morning and evening stretch exercises that she found online. When the day arrived that a door would open, she decided she would walk through it looking her best.

When that breakthrough came, it came on a day that dawned no differently from any other. As usual, it began with some early morning stretch exercises, the smell of coffee and the squeals of *Oui Oui* on the TV. Janique dropped off her daughter at nursery, and was on her way to work when a text message arrived from Roland, asking if they could meet this evening: something significant had happened that he could not discuss by phone. Janique asked if he would mind meeting in her neighbourhood, and if she could bring her children along as she had no childcare after nursery. Meeting at her apartment was out of the question, so she suggested a bistro nearby. Roland agreed.

When they met that evening, Roland explained that their marketing manager had resigned and he offered Janique the job if she wanted it. Within a week, Janique had resigned her secretarial job, and was getting ready to move. It all seemed so surreal. Almost untrue.

Giving back

Janique now runs an online 'job club' for those who are ensnared as she once was. Many of them are mothers of young children, time-trapped as well as money-trapped in cul-de-sacs formed by shifting economic patterns outside their control. When she recounts her own experience, and talks about those months lost in a sense of failure and isolation, this often strikes a very emotional chord.

She's certainly not isolated now. Though she spends less time in restaurants than in her former professional life, she gets real fulfilment from renewed contact with her friends, and deep appreciation from the online job-club members. She runs a weekly conference call where each week she guides participants through yet another of the seven gateways to courage.

When she tells her story, she places equal emphasis on the courage as on the asking. If she had not asked Roland for support, she would have never received that message, and would have never known about that vacancy. And if she had not actively worked on her courage, she would have never renewed contact with Roland in the first place.

Janique encourages members of the job club to abandon resentment and blame, and instead to focus on those things that they can control, the small everyday steps to self-care, friendship, self-discipline and purpose that build courage. In particular, she challenges the members with the 'courage to ask': to let people know what's happening and to make specific requests for help.

COURAGE-BUILDING TIPS FOR JOBSEEKERS

Avoid over-preparation. You are not responsible for how you are heard. You are only responsible for asking, not the outcome.

Make an extra call every day.

Complete this sentence: 'The reason I'm calling is…'

Create a reason that you can call anyone. This can be some

research you are doing, feedback you have had, or facts you want to check. Make this about *them*, not about *you*. Ask for introductions. Be as specific as possible: 'Who else do you know – perhaps in pharmaceuticals – whose feedback I should get on this?'

Pick 'top three' tasks every day, and do them. Do them before lunch, if possible. You will feel so good about yourself; you will do even more in the afternoon!

19

Karl gets a Surprise

'Be harsh with yourself at times' – Seneca

The D-day for which Karl had been anxiously waiting finally arrived. Much as he feared, the axe fell. His employers advised him of impending redundancy, to be supported with an outplacement package to help him find a new job.

Karl was almost relieved. The anxiety of the past few months had taken its toll, and at least he now knew what was going to happen. He could make his own plans. Far from feeling a victim of circumstance, he felt in charge of his own decision-making.

The first thing that Karl decided was that he didn't want another job; he decided to go freelance. The life of an independent professional held a lot of appeal, and he would never again have to spend anxious months worrying that his future lay in other people's hands. With his programme-management experience, together with confidence in his eventual ability to open doors (even if this ability had yet to be proven), Karl decided that he had what it took to be successful as an independent.

Reflecting on the 'courage to ask', Karl decided to ask his employers for two things. First, he explained that he was planning to go freelance, so he asked if he could spend the outplacement budget on specialist business coaching for independents. He didn't want advice about reformatting his CV; he wanted to build a specialist professional identity in an international marketplace.

The HR manager explained that the outplacement company offered this service too, but when Karl probed their experience in this area (more 'asks'), it proved to be lightweight, particularly around the challenges of building an international reputation. So Karl held out, and eventually negotiated a slightly higher severance package that left him free to make his own arrangements.

Karl's second request was that his employers consider him for an initial contract: ideally two to three days per week. He pointed out that they would need assistance while they were making people redundant, that his continuing appearance with a number of key clients would be reassuring, and that either party could terminate the arrangement at a month's notice.

His employers saw the logic of this, but still seemed uncertain. Sensing their hesitation, Karl asked, 'What is your biggest worry about this?' to which they (eventually) admitted their concern that Karl might use this opportunity to do business development for himself and steal some of 'their' clients. Once this issue was on the table, it was easy to resolve within the terms of a confidentiality agreement, and Karl felt satisfied that he had persisted in his courageous questioning.

So far, so good. Despite the setback of redundancy, Karl felt he was making good use of all seven gateways. He analysed his scores and characteristics:

His OCEAN Characteristics: Consistent, Efficient and Organised, Outgoing, Challenging, Assured

GATEWAY	Initial Score (How he felt)	Accessibility Score	Based on Characteristics of… (see Chapter 9)
Connection to others	4	1	Outgoing
Purpose and Meaning	3	3	Consistent, Efficient, Challenging
Influence and Communication Skill	1	4	Consistent, Efficient, Outgoing, Assured
Self-awareness	2	3	Efficient, Outgoing, Assured

Self-discipline	4	4	Consistent, Efficient, Challenging, Assured
Curiosity and Creativity	3	3	Outgoing, Challenging, Assured
Physical Stamina	4	5	Consistent, Efficient, Outgoing, Challenging, Assured

He could easily relate to the gateways of Purpose and Meaning, Self-discipline, Curiosity and Creativity, and Physical Stamina. The two 'social' gateways, however, presented an interesting paradox. While Karl felt he had a good sense of Connection to Others, this gateway didn't score very highly for him. On the other hand, although he didn't feel he was influencing and communicating very well, this third gateway did appear to fit well with his personality characteristics. How could this be? What did this mean?

Many people would ignore a puzzle like this, but Karl couldn't let it go. Somehow it seemed relevant to his current situation, though he couldn't put his finger on how or why.

Feast and famine

In any case, there was little time for reflection. Karl was busy adapting to the new arrangements. He enjoyed creating his own business identity and logo, even if he was barred from using this brand with the clients of his former employer. He engaged a business coach with specialist experience supporting independent professionals to obtain work internationally. He constructed his own website, and wrote some articles about programme management.

The three days per week of delivery soon moved to four and then to five. Karl was delighted that his income was now exceeding what he had previously earned as an employed programme manager. His coach seemed less thrilled, however, and warned Karl he was moving into the risk area of 'feast and famine', by being in delivery mode all the time, and therefore having no dedicated time to develop his own business.

Karl was not concerned. With his usual assurance, he was confident that he was 'making hay while the sun was shining'. He was building financial reserves; business development and the cultivation of opportunity could afford to wait. He got his website done, wrote some articles on programme management and was relentless with his planning and organisation. It was satisfying to see his own work – with his own logo – on his own site. Karl felt he had arrived: he had his own sense of identity, he was making more money than ever and all the gates to courage seemed open.

When two of the assignments ended, Karl took his family on a well-earned holiday to Indonesia, then returned to work… and an unusually empty diary. Within a month, he suddenly found he had switched from 'feast' to 'famine'. His former state of near-overwhelm had now given way to a state of insecurity. For the first time ever, Karl had an entire calendar month in front of him where he knew in advance he would be paid zero.

Suddenly, Karl felt his confidence evaporating. Back from holiday, he now found it hard to make calls or attend social occasions. He would sometimes register for these events, and then invent a last-minute excuse for not going. Though aware of what he was doing, he seemed powerless to prevent it happening. What was happening to his confidence? The gateways to courage seemed to be clanging shut one after another. Procrastination (not even of the sophisticated variety) seemed to be taking over and he seemed powerless to stop it.

He tried to access courage via a greater awareness of his achievements and strengths (fourth gateway) and found that he couldn't. His current inability to open doors was a vivid reminder of his previous struggle with business development when he was employed, and Karl suddenly realised that all his courage was predicated on results. Now that the results were again in question, Karl felt his courage deserting him.

He still loved his family and they loved him. But he couldn't see how this sense of connection was going to translate into that first gateway to courage. Work was entirely another domain. As for strengths, yes, he had plenty, but how come nobody was calling him up asking for them? That fourth gate seemed invisible, perhaps even closed.

His sense of purpose (second gateway) seemed to be still intact: to build a successful independent business. But just now this seemed to be so hard. Would he have to struggle with this 'hustle' for business, year after year? Despite his confidence in his abilities, his self-discipline and his stamina, life before him looked like a long, hard slog.

Karl looked out the window at the cold and rain, and ruefully reflected that even his physical courage seemed to be deserting him. Just now he couldn't even motivate himself to go for a run. As for learning communication skill, he just couldn't be bothered. In any case, what skills? Thinking of all the skills he had to date, Karl found it hard to see what value they now had.

Even as he acknowledged the downward slide into self-pity, Karl felt powerless to stop it. He used to joke about people who were victims or martyrs. 'Get off the cross, they need the wood.' Now, it somehow didn't seem so funny.

The current of discouragement seemed very strong indeed. The will to ask anyone for anything just didn't seem to be there. The effort needed to collaborate just seemed to be too much.

Even fear wasn't enough. Karl imagined a life without holidays, in debt, feeling that sense of failure that Janique described. If anything, this only discouraged him more. He wondered if he was suffering from depression, if perhaps he should seek a doctor and maybe even take medication.

All gateways seemed closed. Perhaps a bit of 'curiosity and creativity' or at least a bit of variety? Another holiday? He dared not spend the money. The outdoors? He hadn't the energy. Night class? Today, he couldn't even bring himself to find the local programme. Wow, this was bad.

Self-awareness

As he reviewed the gateways idly, Karl's eye caught sight of the paradox he had noted earlier. Was he really connecting with others, or just going through the mechanics of keeping in touch? Was there something about his communication style that he needed to learn?

Janique kept coming to his mind. He pictured her still in that high-rise apartment, surrounded by kids' toys, exhausted after her day's work, checking that the steel door was locked when there were shouts on the stairwell. Would that be his fate too?

Karl wondered how Janique was getting on. Out of curiosity, he emailed her. He candidly described his own sense of failure, how he could not bring himself to take action, how all gateways seemed locked or invisible or else leading nowhere. He wished her well and hoped that her secretarial job was still intact.

Janique's reply was a bit of a surprise. What was perhaps most surprising was a frank paragraph that told Karl to stop pretending and abandon his shell of smug confidence. Janique was forthright: 'I don't think any less of you for your suffering today, than I thought more of you when you were awarding yourself points for achievement beforehand. Karl, you are not your results. Get off the cross, they need the wood… remember? If you could let go of your own agenda, more people might want to see you.'

Karl had not expected that. If he had imagined a reply at all, he had imagined someone who would understand his sense of failure and echo that. This Janique had long left her secretarial job and was established in a new apartment, yet she seemed to have brought the strength of survival with her. Plus a power in direct communication that Karl had not anticipated.

He began to realise that his own communication had been obsessed with himself and his own plans, projects and achievements. When he kept in touch with people, it was with his own interests in mind. Even with Janique, he was looking for sympathy; someone whom he thought would give him understanding. Instead, she had given him a challenge.

Karl realised he had some learning to do, and asked his coach for help to improve not only his communication style, but also the mindset that was driving both his frustration and disappointment. He realised he was coming across as self-obsessed because he was too focused on his own agenda, and he began to understand that despite all the frenzy of keep-in-touch activities, he was not connecting with people as well as he thought he was.

His coach congratulated him on a difficult moment of self-awareness. It was a hard pill to swallow, but Karl had hopes it would be more beneficial than the prescription medication he had been contemplating only a few days earlier.

Ask vs tell

Together with his coach, Karl began to apply his new self-awareness to his business development activities and conversations. He consciously revised his keep-in-touch calls so that they were more about the other person than himself. He began to formulate questions about their successes more than their shortfalls or even their needs. When the temptation arose to offer advice or his expertise before it had been solicited, he consciously resisted these impulses.

To begin with, these calls felt a bit odd. But Karl quickly noticed some benefits. First, once he got the hang of it, these calls were a lot easier to make. He didn't have to be forearmed with an offer or something interesting to say. Second, the balance of talking to listening changed dramatically. Because Karl was leading with questions (rather than viewpoints or messages), he was talking less and listening more.

Third, his curiosity was stimulated. As he stopped trying to be interest**ing**, and instead focused on being interest**ed**, he found that he really was getting more curious and open to what was happening in the marketplace. He was learning. He found that he was not alone; many others were battling with the same transition – even entire companies were relearning how to talk to their customers.

Work in progress

Real life is not Hollywood, and this story does not have a conventional happy ending. At least, not yet. Karl is still looking for an assignment, but at least he's enjoying life along the way. He is back running and visiting the gym. Every day he is connecting with people to a depth that he never did before. He is discovering a sense of humour that he didn't know he had.

Karl's purpose has not changed: he still wants to build a successful freelance business. His coach is encouraging, reminding Karl that he is training for a marathon, not a sprint. His second round of research has proved particularly fruitful recently, and he is now opening doors at senior level in ways that he never managed to open before.

As his coach often reminds him, it's now that Karl is meeting the real test of courage. Anyone can feel courageous when the results are good, the money is flowing in, and clients are calling up. But the real test of courage happens when the chips are down, when the results are as yet uncertain. It takes courage to detach from one's agenda and laugh: to 'mock the imposters' of success and failure (Kipling). This is when the muscles of courage are often developed.

Who needs an experienced programme manager with a good sense of humour?

COURAGE-BUILDING FOR INDEPENDENT PROFESSIONALS

Each week consists of three types of time: delivery time, development time and admin time. You neglect one of these at your peril. Karl didn't heed the warning: do you have the courage to do so?

- Your weekly development plan has five headings. All involve asking.
- **Current clients**: exploring *their* opportunities, threats, needs, imperatives – not *yours*
- **Referrals**: who (and how) can you ask for introductions?
- **Keeping in touch**: individual 'asks' are usually better than broadcast emails
- **Strategic alliances**: what can you ask, together with them?
- **Your showcase**: website, social media, using results from your research. Who else can use this? How can this extend your reach?

In negotiating project fees, there are four stages of asking, ideally in this order:

- The **work** to be done, why is this important?
- The **resources**, including budget, who has these?
- The **fee**. You cannot charge a fee if you cannot ask for it.
- Other aspects of the **agreement**, for example, what will they need to do to make this a success?

As an independent, your destiny is in your hands. Economies may experience a downturn; but an individual professional does not have to. Karl's story is not yet over.

(Further information for independent professionals: see www.success121.com)

20

Maria Rediscovers

'Really Hagrid, if you are holding out for universal popularity, I'm afraid you will be in this cabin for a very long time.' – J. K. Rowling, Harry Potter and the Goblet of Fire

Once she examined each gateway, Maria found it easy enough to name what was missing. The gap stood out like a great void in the middle of an otherwise full life:

Her OCEAN Characteristics: Curious, Efficient and Organised, Outgoing, Adaptable, Assured

GATEWAY	Initial Score (How she felt)	Accessibility Score	Based on Characteristics of... (see Chapter 9)
Connection to others	2	3	Curious, Outgoing, Adaptable
Purpose and Meaning	1	1	Efficient
Influence and Communication Skill	3	5	Curious, Efficient, Outgoing, Adaptable, Assured
Self-awareness	2	5	Curious, Efficient, Outgoing, Adaptable, Assured
Self-discipline	2	2	Efficient, Assured

Curiosity and Creativity	4	4	Curious, Outgoing, Adaptable, Assured
Physical Stamina	3	3	Efficient, Outgoing, Assured

Despite her numerous achievements, Maria could not find any meaning in what she was doing. All other gateways to courage scored higher in terms of accessibility, as indeed they were. She had no difficulty communicating, she was aware of her emotional state and of her capacity to manage this herself even in stressful situations. She was creative, adaptable and well-connected with others. She had both stamina and self-discipline, and at the same time she was open to experience.

But *for what?* This was the great unanswered question in her life, the big void in a fertile valley of achievement. What was the meaning of it all? Throughout all the waves of reorganisation, the complexity of a global role, what was important enough to give a sense of significance and consequence to all her efforts?

When she retired some day, or found herself being 'managed-out', on what could she look back with pride, knowing she had made a difference?

She had chosen a career in Human Resources for its 'human' element, but found that the 'resources' dimension had taken over. Maria found herself lurching from one initiative to the next. As wave after wave of reorganisation struck the boat, she was trying to navigate the latest direction, while trying to keep herself and others afloat at the same time. As well as keeping an eye on the destination, she had to watch out for changing currents, the welfare of the crew and the force of the wind.

She had too many 'purposes' but not enough meaning. Maria had no problem with single-mindedness or goal-setting. She could prioritise and achieve. She had always been inwardly motivated to excel. But meaning was another matter. How were her current projects valuable and really making a difference?

In all the flurry of goal-setting, the second gateway of meaning had become obscured, even forgotten. The ivy grew around it, making the gateway invisible and even spreading to other gateways so that courage was becoming less and less accessible. Her achievements seemed less significant; her strengths seemed to be of less value. So what if management ratings were improving? It was all just a game, anyway and a hectic game, at that. Played at lightning speed. There was little time for reflection about meaning.

Yet without a sense of meaning, collaboration had become a necessary chore rather than a pleasure. Maria recognised that she was having out-of-body-experiences during meetings: watching herself go through the motions of consultation and inclusion around decisions that had already been taken. The falsity of the role-play was distasteful, but 'it had to be done'. If not her, someone else would be doing it.

Maria noticed that she was using these phrases more and more. Not just to herself, but also to the country HR managers, who often had to be motivated to implement initiatives about which they were obviously less than enthusiastic. Indeed, the more she thought about it, Maria was shocked to find that she was frequently trying to motivate people to do things that, at best, she only half believed in, and about which they too were politely sceptical.

And now there was this meeting in the US next week about headcount reduction, another storm brewing to rock the boat. She would be busy for the months ahead, coordinating a set of initiatives across countries, checking compliance with local labour law, reallocating budgets and competency transfer. Not to mention managing communication so that nothing leaked at the wrong moment. Her heart sank as she thought about it.

Why not just resign? She was tempted. Both Maria and her husband were financially independent, or nearly so. They could downsize and cut a lot of expenditure. Maria was sure she could get herself an occasional consulting job, a bit like Karl. Her CV was impeccable. Perhaps she could find another job in an organisation whose values were more in line with hers?

But what were these values, really? She used to use words like 'inspiration', 'excellence' and 'contribution' but how empty these words now seemed. Worse still, they were frequently used to camouflage some very prosaic realities. 'Business excellence' had become another term for 'cost cutting'. Your 'contribution' was how well you were hitting your targets. And Maria was all too aware that those targets were not primarily designed with 'inspiration' or 'meaningfulness' in mind.

Maria had imagined that a global HR role would be like the bridge of a ship: where enlightened people would gather, gaze at the horizon and imagine exciting journeys on which to take the passengers and the personnel. The reality was more like the purser's office: dealing with admin, resources and passing messages between crews.

Give it up and have a life?

Leaving all this behind held a lot of appeal for Maria. She had been doing it long enough. It would not be a popular decision, but she would not be very popular after next week's US meeting anyway. Popularity was the least of her worries.

So what held her back? Why not just write the letter of resignation, and hand it to Bob next week in the US? Or better still, produce it publicly in the meeting? Maria smiled as she imagined the flurry that would cause. She felt sorely tempted.

Yet something didn't feel right. What was that? Financial insecurity? No, not really. A bit of apprehension there, but money was not a show-stopper. Being at home? No, she would be able to spend more time both with her daughter and her mother, and therefore would feel less guilty. David would be happy. No, it wasn't that.

It was more a feeling of 'giving up'. If everyone who cared about what was happening were to just resign and depart, that would just leave the floor to those who were playing the system for their own career and benefit. Yes, they were probably in the majority already, but at least were held in check by the necessity of dealing with those who had aspirations beyond their own immediate bonuses.

The more that Maria thought about that, the more she felt she couldn't leave. She could however deal with being fired, if dealing with that became necessary. She would at least be fired in defence of her values, and she could live with that.

Decisions, decisions

But what about her family? Was it fair to subject them to all of this?

Maria realised that these choices would be complex, as indeed would the resulting course of action. She needed to find someone to help her navigate this maze. But who? Her friends didn't know her world. Neither did professionals like Karl or Graham: while they knew the world of business, they were not at senior level in global organisations like hers. What had she read recently that might be useful?

Her mind went back to a blog she had been forwarded about collaborative leadership. The author had worked in investment banking for many years, and he had written an interesting article about how risk was better managed by leaders collaborating with each other rather than controlling each other. In particular, he had described a key problem that Maria immediately recognised: collaboration necessitated leaders having the courage to give up *control*, which many of them just couldn't do. You cannot collaborate if you always insist on having the final decision.

One of the reasons the article had struck a chord with Maria was that she realised that she herself had difficulty giving up control. She liked to figure out the answer first, and then communicate the end-product – in that order. She saw she was even doing this right now in her battle to find meaning.

Perhaps she could use some of her stronger gateways in order to discover this elusive one? Using the gateway of Self-awareness, she could see that she was battling alone. To build more courage (as opposed to more control), it was time to do some collaboration about herself and her own needs.

She eventually located the blog and contacted the author, whose name was Philippe. She explained she wanted a mentor/ thinking-partner for the months ahead, and asked him about his experience of working with executives. In his deceptively soft voice, Philippe asked some edgy questions of his own that courteously interrupted Maria's (rather controlling!) interview and got her thinking. She relished the challenge, and soon they were working together exploring current developments on collaborative leadership, and how this might apply both to her current dilemma and the organisation for which she worked.

It came as no surprise to discover that the first person that Maria had to lead in this way was herself. She and Philippe had quite a few laughs about their initial 'interview'. Collaboration meant working together to resolve issues, not presenting people with finished solutions or criteria and then trying to engage them to implement. This meant making space for the 'unresolved' – even protecting this space long enough to allow creative thinking to develop. It meant resisting the temptation to manipulate the process in order to get others believing they had co-created the solution that you had already decided was right for them. Ouch! This was all too familiar.

By working with Philippe, Maria decided not to create any drama in the US meeting, but to be as collaborative as the situation allowed. In particular, she resolved to work on herself, as she recognised that leaving space for the uncontrolled (and uncontrollable) was not exactly her intuitive way of working. Up until now, she had driven high standards by exerting control. It seemed almost cavalier to give this up.

Collaborative leadership

Maria also resolved to introduce collaborative leadership to her company, by stealth at first. At every opportunity, she presented a contrast between 'command and control' and 'collaboration' and asked (as neutrally as she could) which route they wanted to follow. She smiled inwardly at the subtle control she was exercising even as she presented this, and realised that this would be a long road even for those who believed in it.

This approach took a fair amount of self-discipline; more than Maria had bargained for. She found herself spending a lot of time and thought around the fifth gateway. Looking at her own team, she could see how some had higher access to self-discipline than others. At one end of the spectrum, one of the country managers had an amazing capacity to execute a short to-do list every day, and could not understand those who didn't or couldn't. At the other end, Maria realised she was spending a lot of time monitoring two others because she did not believe anything they said.

Together with Philippe, Maria explored how self-discipline would be vital both to her own sense of courage and the organisation's use of collaboration. Collaboration meant trust, and trust in turn meant reliance. How can you rely on someone who does not have self-discipline? If they lack that essential bridge from intention to action, from enthusiasm to execution, then the success of collaboration would be short-lived. No wonder many leaders preferred control to collaboration.

At times this way of working was messy, and it was very tempting to go back to a much more controlling style of leadership. Yet Maria could see the potential to build genuine engagement with her team, and she could see how this was enhancing her strongest gateway, Influence and Communication Skills. Most importantly, she had found something meaningful, even if it was the early days of discovery.

There were encouraging little victories along the way. Maria's burden of work lightened as she delegated a bit more to the country managers. Even the dreaded headcount-reduction wasn't as bad as she feared, partly because she accepted there were aspects of this that nobody could control, such as losing some good people that the organisation didn't want to lose.

There were setbacks, too. She faced resistance, just as Philippe had warned her. Many managers had been brought up on a diet of command and control, and would not ever be willing to shift from 'individual success' to 'shared success'. Some would always be driven by the 'look at me!' style of leadership. There would be brick walls, but as Randy Pausch has said: 'The brick walls are there to give us a chance to show how badly we want something'.

With the support of Philippe, Maria was *asking* more, and controlling less. She was getting groups of people together to really make decisions, as opposed to coming up with decisions that had already been made. She was asking genuinely open questions, like: 'Why is this important?' She encouraged her managers to become more familiar with the business: for example, to sit alongside people and work *with* them for a day rather than bouncing a job description over and back by email.

As a collaborative approach caught hold, there were some surprising results. Some of these results were hard to swallow. For example, the country managers discovered that many of the 360-degree feedback sessions were often much resented: dreaded by both parties as superficial judgements about the work, rather than sharing a genuine understanding of the work. This meant a complete revision of the appraisal mechanism: with a completely different set of questions that focused on *how* one's work was valuable, rather than how valuable it was. 'Fewer adjectives, more outcomes' became an unofficial slogan.

Other gateways

As Maria got immersed in a renewed sense of meaning, other gateways opened up. Her physical energy had always been good, and this was now boosted by a job that had meaning. Maria could apply her strengths and communication skills to problems, whether they were difficult challenges or boring tasks, and in turn she noticed her self-discipline to be higher than ever.

She was no longer building a wall, but a 'cathedral' where collaborative leadership became a collective learning journey. Despite resistance in many quarters, Maria is now encouraged by pockets of success. In particular, those teams who have to do collaborative bidding and proposal writing with external partners have become strong advocates for the work Maria is doing. The results are encouraging.

At home, too, Maria finds she can be more 'present' to her family. While her husband had rarely complained about her business travel, or absence from home, he used to get annoyed when Maria was preoccupied at mealtimes and obviously worrying about work-related things. Now that the void is less evident, the dinner table is also more relaxed. In her home life, Maria has found that collaboration works too, as long as the mind and body are really there. As her husband had always said, it's not the quantity of time she spends at home; it's the quality of that time that counts.

In all areas, Maria is still learning to let go, and not to struggle with 'resistors' too much. Sometimes this is hard, for example, with a finance director who seems hell-bent on sabotaging her every initiative. She is often frustrated that she has to spend so much time managing his interference, and it galls her to think that he enjoys it. At times like this, it's vital that she has a sense of meaning to fall back on. When all other gates close, or become invisible, this one is always accessible.

So is working with others (the first gateway). Collaboration has brought deeper relationships at every level; 'almost human' as Maria once said to Philippe. The words had escaped before she saw the tragicomic side. Maria is fortunate to have a good friend in finance who keeps her quietly appraised of what the FD is up to. They can both discuss their uneasy feelings that they are indulging in precisely the type of behind-the-scenes politicking that ideally they would like to get rid of.

However imperfect, there is nevertheless a sense of connection in their shared vision. They accept the realities of an imperfect world. In the words of Ethylios: 'To be perfect is to accept expanding imperfection.'

THE COURAGE TO ASK FOR LEADERS

- What conversations are you avoiding? With whom? Why?
- Are your open questions really open? (What, Where, How, Why...) Or is there a 'right answer'?
- Are you exploring how their work is valuable, or how valuable it is? What's the difference?
- Do you make clear requests, or do you manage by insinuation? (How do you know?)
- To what extent are you collaborating? Or is collaboration just a tool for influencing others?
- Are you asking for what you need? What do you need?
- With whom can you safely explore unfinished ideas or troubling questions?

'ASKS' THAT COURAGEOUS LEADERS CAN MAKE

- If there were no 'right answer', what would you say is the principal benefit of... (problem with... etc.)?
- Who should I be spending more time with? How? When? Why is that important?
- May I ask you to... The ideal result would be... (making requests in terms of both task and outcome).
- Today, I'm asking that we table all our concerns about x. Let's not judge them or fix them, let's just get it on the table, and hear why this is important.
- If there was just one thing you could change, what would it be? How would you know it had changed?
- What have we not talked about, that we should have?

21

Graham gets Curious

'Curiosity is the wick in the candle of learning'
– William Arthur Ward

With his customary scepticism, Graham eyed up each of the gateways with no great sense of confidence. Being more easy-going than the others, it took considerable effort even to put his scores together. Nevertheless he did – if somewhat languidly and disinterestedly, as if he were doing sudoku.

His OCEAN Characteristics: Curious, Easy-going, Solitary, Challenging, Sensitive.

These characteristics bore out a hunch that Graham had had ever since his university days: that he was a mass of contradictions. Life often seemed to be much easier for other people. Some of these people might be challenging and assured (as opposed to sensitive, like himself), so they worried less. Others were both easy-going and outgoing, or perhaps just naturally consistent (as opposed to being incessantly curious and easily bored, as he was). Either way, most people seemed less conflicted.

Graham suspected that many others did not suffer as he did. Despite his easy-going nature, despite taking life as it came, he sometimes wondered if he was composed out of a cocktail of ingredients that did not sit easily together. His curiosity was piqued and Graham looked at the gateways:

GATEWAY	Initial Score (How he felt)	Accessibility Score	Based on Characteristics of: (see Chapter 9)
Connection to others	1	3	Curious, Easy-going, Sensitive
Purpose and Meaning	1	3	Solitary, Challenging, Sensitive
Influence and Communication skill	1	2	Curious, Easy-going
Self-awareness	blank	3	Curious, Solitary, Sensitive
Self-discipline	0	2	Solitary, Challenging
Curiosity and Creativity	0	5	Curious, Easy-going, Solitary, Challenging, Sensitive
Physical Stamina	0	2	Easy-going, Challenging

Graham's eye wandered from gateway to gateway. Connection to Others and Purpose and Meaning seemed to be recommended, but he could not see himself doing much with these right now. Yes, he wished he had both of these, but he didn't. As for Self-awareness and Self-discipline', Graham ruefully reflected that if he had more of these qualities, he would not be in this mess in the first place.

The gateway of Curiosity clearly stood out. At least this one held some attraction. Heeding the advice to start wherever is easiest – which Graham always did, anyway, if indeed he started at all – he wondered if he might explore this gateway a bit further.

There was no doubt that he was bored. He was bored with his clients, his practice and even Hannah's concerned looks. He was fed up with his financial problems. He was tired of chasing clients for payment. Most of all, he was bored with those feelings of failure, of wasted potential.

So what could he do to liven up his life a little? He didn't want to join clubs and start meeting people: that might be OK for extroverts, but deep down Graham was shy and he didn't feel he had the energy for that right now. Joining a gym or a cycling club didn't appeal either. Sure, he could go off on his own, walking or cycling, but wouldn't that just leave him ruminating in solitude about his own miserable state?

Arriving home at his flat, Graham picked up the local paper from a pile in the hallway and while microwaving his evening meal, started idly flicking through the pages. More boring pages of adverts, classifieds and arguments between local councillors. Yet Graham's eye was caught by a tiny paragraph about a new drama club that was meeting in a few days to audition for Tom Stoppard's play *Arcadia*.

Why not? Graham had been highly regarded as an actor in his university years. The drama society had often provided his escape from the anxiety of exams. So the following Tuesday found Graham reading the part of the flamboyant Bernard Nightingale and was instantly cast – not without a certain irony, he reflected – in the same self-absorbed role.

Within a few weeks, Graham was having fun and Hannah soon noticed the change. That old wicked smile was back and there was occasional humour again in the office. And in that lighter vein, Graham suggested that Hannah and he go to lunch one day, and discuss how they could pull in some more clients and cash. Hannah was relieved, as the figures she was currently preparing were more worrying than ever.

Over lunch, she chose to share some of these worries with Graham. He admitted that he didn't have instant answers, but was determined to find them and to pull in some new business as quickly as possible. He asked Hannah for her suggestions. She proposed that they take a half-day to review everything they had tried to date, and decide on the best approach together.

Both Hannah and Graham felt better after that lunch. At least the problem was out in the open. And Graham couldn't help noticing that the first gateway (Connection with Others, in this case with Hannah) was also opening a bit – even though he hadn't consciously been trying. And it felt good.

Perhaps he would even tell her about these gateways. Mmm. Maybe next time.

Asking

Before that, he needed to tackle that Law Society complaint. Thinking about the 'courage to ask', he decided to ask a colleague to represent him, and to be open about his difficulty paying for this. From his own legal work, Graham was well aware that it's all too difficult to get true perspective on one's own problems. 'The lawyer who represents himself has a fool for a client', as the old adage puts it. He felt a bit embarrassed, but he asked anyway, and was relieved when his colleague recommended someone who had a lot of experience in handling these complaints. Another bit of Connection, the first gateway nudged open a bit more.

But all of this would eventually have to be paid for, and that meant getting new clients, fast.

During a half-day review with Hannah, Graham shared what he had been learning about *asking*: that most of their initiatives to date had been stuck in 'broadcast-mode' and that when it came to developing opportunity, what they needed to do was to *ask more*. Together they wrote a list of how they could do this:

- **Asking for referrals** and recommendations; which had always been their best source of business, anyway (Action: Graham/Hannah)
- **Asking some potential introducers** to lunch, e.g. accountants (Action: Graham)
- **Asking where Graham could give a talk**, and use those storytelling skills of his to entertain an audience (Action: Hannah to research opportunities)
- **Asking former clients** if they would be willing to be interviewed, for a website or a possible newsletter (Action: Graham and Hannah)
- **Asking new clients** where they had first heard about the firm (Action: Graham)
- **Asking for slightly higher fees** and prompt payment (Action: Graham)

- **Asking about local networking events,** which either Hannah or Graham could attend (Action: Hannah)
- **Asking editors** to publish occasional articles (Action: Hannah)

They decided to stop there, as this was already too much to do. Nevertheless, they acknowledged that they could go on, and that probably more innovative 'ask-ideas' were yet to come.

Self-discipline

This was all very well, but would it ever happen? It's easy to write a list, but it takes real self-discipline to start doing what's on the list. Knowing Graham, Hannah was unsure how to raise this subject. He could be very tetchy on that score.

Yet if the 'courage to ask' was to mean anything, the question had to be asked. Otherwise all the other 'asks' would probably never happen. And then all would be lost, anyway.

So, as diplomatically as she could, Hannah took the bull by the horns: 'Graham, what might get in the way of us actually doing these things?'

The silence that followed Hannah's question seemed very long. She wondered if she had gone too far. Graham could have a fragile ego sometimes; he could so easily take offence.

When he answered, Hannah was surprised. Thoughtfully, he said 'I could… get bored… by the asking. I won't find it easy to ask every new client where he heard about us. I will "forget" to ask for introductions. This is all going to take a degree of self-discipline.'

As he said the word 'discipline', Graham remembered the fifth gateway. He had not scored very highly there, yet he remembered that a modicum of self-discipline would always be needed to bridge from thought to action. Perhaps it was time to apply this now.

The time had come to tell Hannah a bit more about the gateways, that all seven were available to everyone, but that he needed particular access to Curiosity and Creativity. And variety too, so he didn't want to lock himself into a rigid regime, this just wouldn't work. He felt that if he could rekindle his desire to win, the self-discipline would follow.

Hannah was not surprised; she already knew Graham and his habits. She was relieved that at last they were talking about the issue. She was impressed by his insight and self-awareness; he had certainly hidden that before. She asked how she could help.

Again, Graham's answer was surprising. He suggested that he was going to retry to 'zone his diary' so that he did the disciplined 'heads-down stuff' in the morning, and tried to leave the afternoons free for meetings, communication and creative stuff. He asked Hannah that he be accountable to her for adhering to this, and that she was not to hold back if she saw him slipping. Hannah agreed, even if she privately wondered how well this would work... and indeed how long it would last.

Business development

Nevertheless, on the whole, their new regime has started to work well. They now have regular weekly meetings every Monday afternoon. Graham had suggested Monday morning, but Hannah was strict with him: mornings were for heads-down stuff, 'taking items *off* lists, Graham, not making new lists'. God, hadn't he unleashed a tyrant here!

The 'tyrant' was also making good use of the seven gateways. Hannah applied the same conscientiousness to her business development activities as she had previously done to her administrative tasks. She called her friend Eileen who worked for the local Chamber of Commerce.

With Eileen's help, she had Graham speak at three different local events, and would not take No for an answer. He was so nervous; she had to drive him to the first one. Yet he was a star, as she knew he would be. With individual people, Graham could be shy, even a bit edgy, but just put him in front of an audience... and watch what happens. What a performer!

Hannah was also doing some networking of her own. The 'courage to ask' didn't stop at getting Graham's permission to do so; Hannah found it relatively easy to do follow-up calls with the people she met, and felt a real sense of pride when she brought her first client: a consultant who wanted to draft an associate agreement. Others soon followed, and now Graham has to start work early every morning, for the simple reason that there is so much to do.

Other gateways

A year on, Graham is a different man. The sense of 'Connection to Others' that started with Hannah has slowly grown into two more friendships: one from the drama club and one of those accountants that he started having lunch with a year ago. The latter shares his wry sense of humour, and bit by bit they have started to share some of their professional challenges with each other, particularly the challenges of creating opportunity. It's good to have a kindred spirit.

Graham's self-awareness has grown, too; particularly his (own brand of) self-discipline. Today, he views self-discipline as an ally that protects his freedom, rather than a jailer that wants to deprive him of liberty and enjoyment. This started with his time-keeping, even on those 'mornings after' following rehearsals. Since then, it's been extended to some bike-riding at weekends, which in turn made him more aware of what he was eating… and drinking.

The big win for Graham has been the discovery that he can do anything he chooses – even when he doesn't *want* to do it. The ability to pick up what's in front of him – whether he feels like it or not – is genuinely new and fascinating. He still would not claim to be 'efficient and organised'; nor does he even aspire to that ideal. But today he is a free man – precisely because he can choose-and-do, as opposed to being a hostage to his mood.

The second gateway of Purpose and Meaning remains a bit of a mystery. Despite the fact that Graham knows this would stabilise his sensitive nature, he has not yet found something that excites him enough. Still, he remains open to that possibility, happy to be curious about those frontiers yet to be explored. The door is open.

THE COURAGE TO ASK FOR PROFESSIONALS
- Which achievements are you most proud of? Why?
- What is the common purpose for which your team is working?
- Who are your loyal collaborators? Why are they loyal?
- How do your best clients find you?
- What do you need to do to stay ahead (and avoid boredom)?

'ASKS' THAT COURAGEOUS PROFESSIONALS CAN MAKE
- Of the work we have been doing together (recap), which aspects have been most useful?

- Why is this important?
- What difference is this making?
- Who else would benefit from support with these issues?
- What's the best way to meet them?
- Whose budget will be supporting this initiative?

22

A Request for You

'When one teaches, two learn' – Robert Heinlein

Everyone wants to make the most of the opportunities that come their way. Many are in search of new openings: careers, markets, jobs.

Perhaps you are one of them. Hopefully this book has helped highlight the significance of 'asking': a daily habit that opens up potential, builds courage and creates opportunity. Asking is more powerful than thinking, planning, reading, reformatting, broadcasting messages... even studying.

But...

The problem is that asking takes courage. Using the seven gateways we have outlined requires more than just reading. There will be many days ahead in which all of us will 'forget' to use them. So the 'courage muscles' start to atrophy and energy levels drop. Then we indulge in 'sophisticated procrastination' to cover up the problem.

What can you do to sustain the growth of courage – even on those days that you don't want to do so?

Request

We ask you to become an (informal) 'courage coach' as soon as possible. By raising other people's game, you will raise your own.

The marketplace has more need of courage now than ever before. In every company, family and organisation, there is uncertainty and anxiety. It takes courage to face these concerns. To date, our culture has favoured the development of *skill* over the development of *courage*. The net result is that many have never developed these vital muscles, and are reaching for another training course or magic solution to solve their problems.

By en-**courage**-ing others, your own courage will develop more rapidly than any course of study we could provide. You don't have to wait to be appointed, or to be asked. You can just begin: right now, in your own family, office, café, anywhere you have a voice.

You can do this formally or informally, individually or in small groups. You can create an 'encouragement group', 'job club', 'referral-club' or anything else that suits your talents and needs.

Objections

'I'm a book-keeper/business analyst/secretary, not a coach.'

'But I've only started to build courage myself!'

'I don't know enough people.'

'It's not the right time.'

No doubt Janique thought many of the same things when she started her job club. You don't even have to start something; there are already many worthy initiatives (in organisations and in neighbourhoods) in need of an encouraging voice.

The best place to begin is in one-to-one conversation. We ask you to have more of these anyway. It won't take long for the subject of courage to come up. Whether it's called 'confidence', 'resilience', 'guts' or something else.

You may use this book in any way you wish. You may send it as a gift to someone who is bravely facing a tough time. You may share it or keep it as your 'secret weapon'; you are free to choose. In any case, you will probably discover some gateways of your own: most people do.

It really doesn't matter, as long as one more person develops *the courage to ask*. This is how opportunity gets cultivated. This is what creates real value.

We wish you well, and look forward to hearing about your progress.

Kate and John

PS: If you would like some useful resources, feel free to email *info@ vco-global.com* and let us know what you are developing.

Part four

23

The Courage to Converse about Value

by Ron Baker

Asking is a crucial skill for those professionals who need to discuss the value of services with clients. Ronald J. Baker is founder of VeraSage Institute and is an international authority on the subject of pricing professional services. We have invited Ron to demonstrate how the courage to ask is a vital skill in professional life.

'Language was invented to ask questions. Answers may be given by grunts and gestures, but questions must be spoken. Humanness came of age when man asked the first question. Social stagnation results not from a lack of answers but from the absence of the impulse to ask questions'
– Eric Hoffer, Reflections on the Human Condition, 2006

Any company that establishes prices based upon value will agree that the conversation with the customer is the most important part of the process. Skipping an in-depth conversation is similar to a contractor attempting to build a customer's dream home without any architectural plans. The better your firm *comprehends* the customer's value drivers, the more likely you will be able to *create* maximum value, *convince* the customer they must pay for that value, and *capture* that value with an effective strategy custom tailored to the customer.

This is an opportunity for you and the customer to create a

shared vision of the future, to analyse where the customer is at this point, and to develop the necessary action plan to move them to where they want to be.

This focus is crucial, because if you do not discuss value with the customer, you will be forced into a discussion of hours, efforts, activities, deliverables and costs, usually by procurement, in-house counsel, or some other professional buyer within the customer's organisation. Remember that the customer is trying to *maximise* the value they receive while attempting to *minimise* your price. It is far more strategic to engage in a discussion over what the customer is trying to maximise rather than what they are trying to minimise. If all you focus on is price, it can never be low enough. If the customer says your price is too high, what they are really saying is, 'I don't see the value in your offering.' It is not a question of money; rather, it is lack of belief.

Naive listening

'When I am getting ready to reason with a man I spend one-third of my time thinking about myself and what I am going to say, and two-thirds thinking about him and what he is going to say' – Abraham Lincoln

Questions require doubt, something professionals who are experts in what they sell are not comfortable with. After all, we are paid to have the answers, not express doubt; and if you already know the answers there appears to be no need to gather any more information from the customer, chaining ourselves to the limits of our existing knowledge.

For this reason, during the conversation the customer should talk at least twice as much as the professional. This is incredibly difficult because it requires self-restraint. Naive listening is difficult because you think much faster than people talk. While someone is talking, you are usually listening with one half of your brain and formulating your answer with the other. Active listening is a skill that needs to be developed.

Talkers may *dominate* a conversation but the listener *controls* it. Taking notes conveys to the customer that what they are saying is important and that you care enough to record it. It also helps you remember exactly what they said. But most of all, and this is precisely why psychiatrists and psychologists take notes, the person will provide much more detail. The more you know, the more value drivers you will be able to uncover, and the higher prices you will command.

You also want to deal with the *economic buyer,* the person who can hire and pay you. Many consultants believe you are wasting your time if you cannot get in front of this person, because most likely you will be dealing with gatekeepers who can only say No, never Yes. This may take a few iterations, but the customer is sending a signal they are not serious if they deny you access to the economic buyer, and you may want to invest your resources in more profitable opportunities, such as servicing existing customers.

Avoid the ever-present temptation to provide solutions to the customer's needs and wants. That is not the purpose of the conversation at this stage. You are on a *value quest* with the customer, not in a venue to begin providing solutions. Your role at this point is to ask questions and have the customer formulate, or at least articulate, a vision of the future. Before doctors *prescribe,* they must *diagnose,* which is the role you must assume at this stage in the conversation. Anything less is malpractice.

Starting the conversation

This is one of the most effective statements to utilise somewhere near the beginning of the conversation, regardless of whether you are meeting with a new or old customer: 'Mr Customer, we will only undertake this project if we can agree, to our mutual satisfaction, that the value we are creating is at least three (to ten) times the price we are charging you. Is that acceptable?'

Do not get sidetracked by the multiple of three to ten, as it will obviously vary from customer to customer. In fact, sometimes you do not need to state a multiple, rather just state that the value needs to exceed the price.

This establishes the right tone near the beginning of the conversation that yours is a firm obsessed with value, along with the willingness to demonstrate the economic impact that your services can have for the customer; how it will improve the customer's life. It also subtly suggests that you will not enter into relationships that do not add value for both parties, the exact tone you want to set, as both sides to a transaction must profit if it is to be sustainable.

The distinction between *needs* and *wants* is important here, as the latter are almost always higher on the value curve than the former. It is more strategic to begin all conversations by leading with customer wants because it is much easier to build a unique value proposition upon them.

Questions you should ask the customer

> *'If all patients were the same, medicine would*
> *be a science, not an art' – Sir William Osler,*
> *one of the fathers of modern medicine*

Something similar to Osler's statement can be said of questioning, it is an art and skill, not a science. Each customer is unique, and so must be your approach to questions. Just as with naive listening, one should not be afraid to take the Lt Columbo approach and ask simple questions. As English mathematician and philosopher Alfred North Whitehead wrote, 'The "silly question" is the first intimation of some totally new development.'

Peter Drucker also taught an effective approach to assignments: approach the problem with your ignorance:

> I never ask these questions or approach these assignments based on my knowledge and experience in these industries. It is exactly the opposite. I do not use my knowledge and experience at all. I bring my ignorance to the situation. Ignorance is the most important component for helping others to solve any problem in any industry.

There are questions you should ask every customer to assist you in determining just where on the value curve your customer is located. The more information you seek from customers, the better equipped you will be to assess their price sensitivity. Always ask open-ended questions to engage the customer in discussing goals, aspirations, fears, desires and dreams of the future. This has a tremendous psychological impact, because most people's favourite topic is themselves. Start with the following questions:

- What do you expect from us?
- What is your business model? How do you make a profit?
- What are your company's critical success factors and key performance indicators (KPIs)?
- How will the services we provide add value to *your* customers?
- Which of our company's offerings is of the highest value to you?
- Who is the next best alternative (competitor) to our company?
- What characteristics do they have that we do not, and vice versa?
- What is your current pain?
- How do you see us helping you address these challenges and opportunities?
- What growth plans do you have?
- If price were not an issue, what role would you want us to play in your business?
- Do you expect capital needs? New financing?
- Do you anticipate any mergers, purchases, divestitures, recapitalisations, or reorganisations in the near future?
- We know you are investing in Total Quality Service, as are we. What are the service standards you would like us to provide you?
- How important is our service and price guarantee to you?
- Why are you changing firms? What did you not like about your former firm that you do not want us to repeat?*
- How did you enjoy working with your former firm?**
- Do you envision any other changes in your needs?
- If we were to attend certain of your internal management meetings as observers, would you be comfortable with that?
- How do you suggest we best learn about your business so we can be more proactive in helping you maximise your business success?
- May our associates tour your facilities?
- What trade journals do you read? What seminars and trade shows do you regularly attend? Would it be possible for us to attend these with you?
- What will the success of this engagement look like?
- What is your budget for this type of service?

*Do not denigrate the predecessor firm. First, this insults the customer and reminds the customer of a poor decision. Second, it diminishes respect and confidence in the profession as a whole.

**Even though the customer is changing firms, almost certainly the customer liked some characteristics of the predecessor. Find out what these were and exceed them. For instance, if they said the prior firm always returned phone calls within one day, return them within four hours.

For tangible value that can be measured and moved from mere evidence to economic impact, here are five questions suggested by Mahan Kalsa:

1. How do you measure it?
2. What is it now?
3. What would you like it to be?
4. What's the value of the difference?
5. What's the value of the difference over time?

If the value is intangible, you can use the above questions and instead of financial measures, have the customer *qualify* the value on a scale of 1 to 10. This will help you prioritise what is really valuable to the customer.

Believing in your worth

Frank Lloyd Wright, at the age of eighty-nine, testified in a trial he was 'the greatest architect in the world'. Afterwards, his wife suggested modesty would have been more effective. Wright replied, 'You forget, Olgivanna, that I was under oath.'

There is great nobility in getting paid what you are worth. Nothing is more satisfying than customers who believe, and act on the premise, that they get what they pay for. The best way to achieve this is to have a value conversation.

(For more about Ron Baker, see 'About the Authors' at the end of this book.)

24

Using LinkedIn to Ask

by Jan Vermeiren and Bert Verdonck

Jan Vermeiren and Bert Verdonck are the bestselling authors of *How to REALLY use LinkedIn*. We invited them to write a guest chapter for The Courage to Ask because social media is such a useful tool for finding new customers or a new job.

LinkedIn is the largest professional network in the world and still growing strong (two new members every second). However, most people don't know what to do with it – even though it is a fantastic tool to find, for example, new customers, employees, partners, experts or a new job.

Frequently, we see people (including so-called 'LinkedIn experts') who believe that they need only a great LinkedIn Profile and then the rest will automatically and magically happen. However, this is not what occurs in reality. Something more proactive is needed.

To see the truth of this, you may wish to ask yourself how often you use LinkedIn to find someone to offer them a job, hire them as a consultant or buy their products? Not so often, right?

In order to really benefit from LinkedIn, something else is needed. A passive presence needs to be transformed into a proactive approach. In this chapter, we map out a five-step basic strategy for success. In the book *How to REALLY use LinkedIn* (which can be downloaded for free: www.how-to-really-use-linkedin.com), you will find more details about each step, and more strategies. The instructions here are correct at the time of writing, but like all software platforms, LinkedIn is constantly changing.

Step 1: Clearly define a specific goal

Take a piece of paper (or whatever you use to write, Word, Notepad, your iPad). Write a goal that can relate to finding new customers, a new job, new employees, partners, suppliers, advertisers, sponsors, volunteers, experts... make it as specific as possible.

Step 2: Think of the people who can help you reach your goal

Reviewing your written goal, it's now important to reflect on 'who are the people in the best position to help me reach my goal?'

At this point, it's useful to expand beyond the people you already know. It is possible to reach anyone in the world via six steps, maximum, so it's worth keeping an open mind and listing the people who are in the best position... even if you don't know them at this stage, or even know their names.

This is a good opportunity to be at your most courageous and imaginative. We will find ways to reach these people later on.

Step 3: Use LinkedIn's 'Advanced Search'

At this point, we suggest you log in to LinkedIn and go to 'Advanced Search' (this is the word 'Advanced' next to the search bar on top of your Home Page). Use the parameters of steps 1 and 2 in the fields available on this page. Looking at these fields might cause you to think of some more parameters for steps 1 and 2 or to change them.

An explanation of all the fields you can use can be found in 'Chapter 7: 10 Strategies to Find People Using LinkedIn' of *How to REALLY use LinkedIn*, but most of them are self-explanatory.

There are now two possibilities: you either find the person or you do not. If you have found the person, go to the next step. If you haven't found this person, the reason might be that he or she doesn't have a Profile on LinkedIn. However, there can be other reasons:

- They filed with a different function from the one you are looking for. For example, maybe you typed in Human Resources Director while this person is profiled as HR Manager. You might need to use different descriptions of a function for a successful search.

· You used other parameters in your search than those in their Profile. Experiment with the options by refining your search on the left-hand side (or change the sort options at the top of the search results). Perhaps they no longer hold the same position any more (change the 'current & past' option for Title) or moved to another company (change the 'current & past' option for Company). Or maybe they listed themselves under a different industry from the one you chose.

Tip: Cast a wide net and fine-tune later on. When applying different parameters, start with the major ones first (for example, country, function, company). If you find any results (big or small), add extra parameters (for example, postal code, industry, language, relationship). This way you can see the effect of some of the parameters you are using. More tips about searching and finding can be downloaded for free from the 'Video & Tools Library' at www.how-to-really-use-linkedin.com.

Step 4: Find people who can help you

If you have too many or too few results of your search, change your parameters on the left-hand side. Then choose the most interesting Profile and look at whom you know in common. You can do this by clicking on 'x shared connections' in the result list (only for second -degree connections) or you can click on someone's name to read their Profile first and then look at whom you have in common on the right-hand side (you may have to scroll down).

If the Profile you are looking at is not what you want, or you are looking for more people, repeat this step.

Remark: If you don't find many second-degree connections (those are the ones you are looking for!), that probably means you don't have a big enough LinkedIn network yet or don't have the *right* LinkedIn network yet. In 'Chapter 5: How to Build Your Network... Fast' in *How to REALLY use LinkedIn* you will receive some tips to build your LinkedIn network quickly.

Step 5: Get introduced to people who can help you

Once you have found the people who can help you reach your goal and your mutual connections, it is time to leave LinkedIn to *ask for an introduction.*

Although you can also use the 'Get introduced through' option on LinkedIn, we don't recommend using it because you don't know how well they know each other. They might have once met at a conference or even just connected with each other without knowing each other personally. If you ask for an introduction via the 'Get introduced through' option, you might wait for a very long time for a reaction, if you get one at all!

Tip: If you insist on using the 'Get introduced through' option, you should know that most of the times your request to your first-degree connection is forwarded to the next person in the chain. Many people are unaware of this and write something (too) personal in the message to the person who will introduce them. For example: let's assume you want to be introduced to the Marketing Manager of Microsoft and you notice that a friend from university is connected to both of you. In your message accompanying your request to be introduced, you mention some of your extra-curricular (going out, drinking, etc.) activities because that's what you have in common. However, your first impression on the Marketing Manager, who can also read those words, will (probably) be your last one!

What's the alternative to the 'Get introduced through' function? This is where 'asking' is a vital skill. Pick up the phone, explain your goal to your mutual connection, and ask how well they know the person you want to reach.

If they don't know them well enough, thank them for their time. If they *do* know them and want to help you, ask them to connect you by introducing you to each other via a *normal email* (not via LinkedIn).

We call this the Magic Mail, and if you want extra tips about this, you are welcome to download them from the 'Video & Tools Library' at www.how-to-really-use-linkedin.com.

Let us clarify this by showing you the difference between using the 'Get introduced through' function and an email outside LinkedIn. If you use the 'Get introduced through' option, *you* need to write a message that can be forwarded by your contact. This is a cold message that is warmed up a bit by your contact. But it is still *you*, a stranger, who wrote the message.

Alternatively, when the person you want to reach on LinkedIn, receives an email from your mutual contact – someone they already *know*, *like* and *trust* to a certain level – they will be much more open to the message. At least, this person will be more open for a conversation with you; at best, you are already 'presold' by your mutual contact.

When we explain the 5-step process in our presentations and workshops, some people tend to object:

'Why do I have to go through these 5 steps? Why does my network not just help me by taking initiatives themselves? They know what I do, so why do I need to ask? And why do I have to follow all the steps, it's less time-consuming for me to send out a mass email.'

The reasons are pretty simple; people are often keen to help each other, but they are so busy with their own personal and professional lives that they don't have the time or energy to start guessing what other people might need.

So your challenge is to trigger them by giving them the right (and specific) input and use the best tools available for each step of the process:

- Find out the connections between people via **LinkedIn**.
- Call your mutual connection over the **phone**.
- Ask to be introduced via an **e-mail**.

Yes, this is more time-consuming than sending out a mass mail. But what do you prefer? Spending less time or getting more results?

The good part about this 5-step process is that it helps people to 'bypass' the most difficult aspect of asking. You don't have to ask a potential customer or employer (or anyone else that can help you reach your professional goals) for an appointment yourself. Instead you ask someone you already know to introduce you. This is not only more comfortable for most people, but also delivers better results: in many cases you are already 'presold' which leads to the other person asking you for more information instead of you having to find the courage to ask them all the time!

Conclusion: Like so much in business and career development, the effective use of LinkedIn hinges crucially on the courage to ask. LinkedIn can help you to identify the people you need to ask, but you have to do the asking.

(For more about Jan Vermeiren and Bert Verdonck, see 'About the Authors' at the end of this book.)

25

Ask for Everything

by Mary Farmer

Mary Farmer is Executive Director of the Talent and Inclusion Strategy Network for Executive Networks, where she connects the enterprise heads of talent, diversity and inclusion from the largest corporations in the world.

In the following (personal) essay, she describes some of the formative influences on her own career, and illustrates the particular significance that 'asking' has for women.

My portfolio career (as business executive, owner and entrepreneur, academic and writer) has taken me around the world, and through a multitude of positions and professions: from managing multilateral development assistance projects in Southeast Asia to Global Director of Diversity and Inclusion for electronics and healthcare giant Philips. My field is organisational behaviour: studying people, organisations and unravelling the *why* behind behaviour.

As Freud famously put so well, 'we hate what we don't understand'. And until we figure out why people do the things they do, we probably won't like it very much. We won't know *how* to ask our key questions, even if we manage to get up the courage to do so.

For many years I had my own cross-cultural and diversity management consulting firm in Europe, global tmc international. It was while I was working as a consultant and trainer for the Royal Tropical Institute (KIT) in Amsterdam that I actually got the 'push' to start my own firm. Attending for the first time what would become my favourite annual event, the Women's International

Networking Conference, held that year (1999) in Milan, I heard brilliant Fast Company author Harriet Rubin speaking about her recent book, *Princessa, Machiavelli for Women*. Now, having been raised by a roving gang of feminists I was not a shy, retiring violet, but like many women was having difficulty deciding what I wanted from life… and then how to ask for it.

Harriet Rubin's message was simple and clear: *Ask for everything*. Women should not hold themselves back from the fray, but rather roll up their sleeves and jump in. Ask for everything from yourself, from life, and particularly from others. The old adage of 'all things come to those who wait' is not only false, it is a good way of ensuring you never get what you want. Don't wait: act. Don't anticipate: ask.

In my work and research on gender and organisations I've seen so many women do truly outstanding work and think, 'they'll notice how devoted and hard-working I am.' No, they won't. If you want the promotion, *ask* for it. Take a note from Susan Jeffries' wonderful book *Feel the Fear and Do it Anyway* ; what's the worst that can happen? They'll say no. Period. Practise in front of the mirror, or with your Labrador retriever, then go out and ask for what you want. It really works.

Harriet Rubin also introduced us to a stunningly effective concept for getting what you want that I have used frequently to great effect: the Rule of Three. When you need something from someone, ask them for three things – two of which are rather difficult or even impossible to provide, the third of which is well within their purview to grant with little effort. And make sure that third request is the one you really want. Say, for instance, you need an extra key to your apartment from your landlord. You ask her for (a) a new oven, (b) bike racks outside the building and (c) a key for your apartment. In gratitude and relief your landlord will always give you the key. Try it, it never fails.

Another Rule of Three that I always apply to consulting projects (to give myself the courage to know which project to accept, and which to turn down) is this one: a project can be *fun*, it can be *lucrative*, and it can be *easy*. Whatever happens, the project should be two of the three. If it's going to be hard, not enjoyable, and not earn you a great deal of money, then don't do it. If it's relatively easy and fun, but doesn't pay too much, probably still going to be worth it. If it's very difficult but also fun and makes you rich – hey, who would say no? This Rule of Three has been an old friend and has never let me down.

Having lived and worked outside my native Canada for most of my career, culture has been a factor of tremendous impact. *how* you ask is easily more important than *what* you ask. An old Golden Rule of sales is that you can sell anything to anyone, you just have to frame it in the right way. The same is true of getting information or input from others.

But a true understanding of culture leads us beyond the Golden Rule. Why should you think that people all expect to be treated the way *you'd* like to be treated yourself? The Platinum Principle provides a better guide – treat others the way *they* would like to be treated. And in order to do this you have to spend real time, energy and effort on understanding why they do the things they do, and what it is they really need. That's a lot of 'asking'!

Of course it's always much easier to treat them according to what *you* want and need instead. This helps explain a lot of mistakes made by business leaders: they assume that what is good for them is also good for others. No, Mr Executive, what's good for you is not necessarily good for your stakeholders, and your way of doing business here is perhaps not going to be universally acceptable.

But I digress. A cautionary tale on the need for both understanding and acceptance of cultural differences: for many years I have been teaching Cross-Cultural Management and Intercultural Communication in MBA schools across Europe. At a prominent Dutch university, as is the norm for MBA schools, groups were formed for project work. One group consisted of several young Dutch and German men, and one young Malaysian woman. Fatimah wore conservative clothing and a headscarf, and was very quiet in the group's meetings. The boisterous and extroverted European men either forgot she was there or shouted over her contributions. Their group performance was mediocre, they were only getting sixes and sevens, and the young men spoke bitterly among themselves about how much better they could be doing with someone other than Fatimah in their group.

Then the first quarter's grades were published: Fatimah had the highest average in the school. By far. She was the most brilliant business student in that year's cohort, perhaps ever. The other members of her group were profoundly shocked and humbled: how much higher could they have been scoring if they had asked Fatimah for her ideas and then really listened to the answers?

The real challenge with cross-cultural communication is the need to go from automatic reflex to reasoned, conscious response. You may not like the way someone does something, you may not agree with it, and you never have to emulate it – but you do have to accord others the right to do things differently than you would do them yourself. Whether or not to follow the cross-culturally competent path should always be a conscious choice, and not based on 'my way is better because… it just is'.

Social media and networks have made it easier than ever to approach total strangers for what we need and want, but in order to be effective we have to approach networking from a spirit of generosity rather than need. 'Give a Gift' is a wonderful way to connect with people. I have always been happy to share my research, presentations, time and contacts with others, because I believe wholeheartedly in karma, and that in order to experience abundance for yourself, you have to also give abundantly to others.

How much easier is it to ask for something if you approach them with a gift? When I contact well-known authors and business gurus to take part in our Executive Networks member events I can tell them with confidence that speaking with our select group of top Fortune 500 executives will give them a unique platform to present themselves as key thought leaders in their area of expertise to real decision-makers. They seldom turn it down.

One of the greatest gifts we can give to others, and receive ourselves, is the Gift of Feedback. Let's be honest… criticism, no matter how tactfully and constructively presented, is never easy to take. Many of us switch into 'defence mode' and do not even hear out those who *dare* to question how or what we are doing. And yet speaking up takes tremendous courage, so even if you do not agree with what you are hearing, you have to be supremely grateful that they care enough about you to take the time, and expend the energy, to tell you about something they think you can improve upon.

The only possible response to receiving feedback and constructive criticism from someone is: Thank you. That's it, nothing else, you can zip your lip. It need never be the cause for anger, defensiveness and, even worse, paranoia and depression. Successful business owners, managers and sporting heroes will all tell you that they benefited profoundly by receiving mentoring, coaching and sponsorship from others inside and outside their organisations. Boris Becker puts it succinctly: 'Feedback is the breakfast of champions.'

Perhaps the hardest thing to do is to accept feedback in the spirit in which it was intended. Don't wait for others to dare to speak up – *ask* for their feedback. Ask what you can improve upon. Ask how others would rate your performance, your contribution. Ask *what* is of value, not just how valuable it is. Open yourself to 360 degree feedback.

This brings us back to our central theme, the courage to ask. I worked with a business coach during the formative years of my company who taught me to reframe my thinking, to stop telling myself 'why would they want me?' and replace it with 'why wouldn't they want me?' This changed inherently the way I approached clients, and also (with Harriet Rubin's voice in the background telling me to 'ask for everything') allowed me to ask others to refer me to their own contacts. This grew my business exponentially, and eventually eliminated the need for cold calls, a process I hated and found generally as unsuccessful as it was unsatisfactory.

'Everything you want is out there waiting for you to ask. Everything you want also wants you. But you have to take action to get it' – Jack Canfield

(For more about Mary Farmer, see 'About the Authors' at the end of this book.)

26

Spiral Dialogue – Talking about Opportunity

by John Niland

> *'Our lives are defined by opportunities, even the
> ones we miss'* – *F. Scott Fitzgerald*

Courage has many applications in the current marketplace: from the specific needs of young professionals to the development of leaders for the future. Not to mention the everyday resilience needed by all, to deal with the challenges of our time.

Nowhere is this so much in evidence as in the field of opportunity creation. Whether this is called 'marketing', 'sales', 'business development' or 'interview skills', both the expertise and the courage needed to succeed are evolving more rapidly than ever before.

If you are that person responsible for next quarter's/next year's pipeline, you are probably aware that times are changing. Conventional 'solution selling', 'consultancy selling', 'strategic selling' and 'whatever-is-latest selling' are all crucially dependent on a mirror activity called 'purchasing'. And the problem is that when purchasing slows down (or hesitates or even stops entirely), it really doesn't matter what the sales strategy is called.

Without 'purchasing', there is not much 'selling'. Many of the B2B sales professionals we now work with are questioning whether the solution-selling techniques taught for decades are still relevant in an age when buying has got more sophisticated. So rather than focus on selling at all, it's perhaps more useful to learn how to facilitate the purchasing process.

So you're building trust... why?

To date, most enlightened business development approaches have centred on the needs of the customer. So far, so good. If you can understand your customer's needs (and their wants, as Ron Baker points out in Chapter 23), you enhance your credibility, you build trust and you increase your chances of winning the contract. (Or job, or funding, or support, or whatever opportunity you are currently seeking.)

Who would argue with that? The only problem is: the prospective customer *knows* this is what you are doing! And so they may be reluctant to accede to requests and to answer questions. Your 'asks' may encounter roadblocks: conscious or subconscious. For example, your prospect may be nervous that you want to 'borrow their watch to tell them the time'... and then charge them for it.

There is a lovely story from the west of Ireland about a farmer rounding up sheep on the Mweelrea Mountains of Mayo. A big Mercedes stops on a lonely stretch of winding road, the rear window rolls down, and the stylish occupant says to the farmer, 'If I can tell you how many sheep you have there, will you give me one?'

The farmer hesitates at this rather strange request, but (scoring highly on 'Openness to experience', see Chapter 9) nods his assent. The gentleman in the car takes out his handheld device, and using the finest in GPS technology, comes up with a precise number within seconds. 'Correct,' says the farmer and, being an honest man, he motions the stylish gentleman to choose a sheep and help himself.

Watching his animal being bundled into the boot, the farmer interrupts, 'By the way, if I can tell you what you do for a living, can I have that animal back?' The gentleman hesitates for a moment, then agrees.

'You're a consultant,' says the farmer. 'How did you know?' says the gentlemen. 'Well,' says the farmer, 'you offered to solve a problem that I didn't have. You told me something that I already knew. And you charged me for all that... Now, can I have my dog back?'

Damage limitation

The problem with a lot of pre-sales dialogue is that the 'farmer' almost expects to be dealing with the above professional: someone who is highly skilled at communication... and equally skilled at arranging subsequent fee-structures for his own benefit. So, how are the following requests likely to be regarded?

To help you with that, it would be good to know more about your strategy. Can we have a meeting to discuss this?

To solve that (technical) problem, we will need to spend more time studying how you operate and talking to some of the managers. Would that be OK?

Would you be willing to take part in a new piece of research we are doing?

Of course, nobody can commit to how long this will take (and hence how much it will cost)... How about we do a study first (for fee =x) and then give you an estimate for the rest?

It's hardly surprising that the farmer puts up some fences, if only to avoid the wholesale plundering of his herd. Many purchasers are now adept at locking down allowed communication between their managers and external advisers.

Shaping the dialogue

To overcome these issues of trust, we now teach our professional clients a technique called 'spiral dialogue'. In short, you don't begin by demanding to know the entire strategy ('top-down approach' in consultative selling); instead you demonstrate credibility by dealing with one specific issue, providing some value up-front, and in doing so winning the right to ask contextual questions. When your customer is ready, you may then spiral outwards, but not before.

For example, let's assume you work in a communications agency and you are asked to design a logo. Conventional 'strategic selling' would probably have you attempt to do the entire marketing strategy; we suggest that your attempts to do so will often *diminish* trust in the eyes of today's sophisticated buyer. However, you can instead ask them essential contextual questions needed to do a logo, ideally using your experience to influence their requirements just a little (also known as reframing or demand-shaping).

So you might ask:

- What prompted you to know that you needed a new logo? What's the problem with the one you have already?
- How will the new logo be used? Who will be seeing it?
- What work have you done so far… for example, to identify the values/criteria that the new logo needs to respect?
- What else is happening that we need to know about, particularly as regards timing, or how the new logo will be used?
- How will you judge that the new logo is being successful? Why is that important?
- We have (three) possible approaches for doing a logo, each with its own budgets, each with different pros and cons. When we are choosing between these options, who do we turn to for advice/direction?
- What can you do yourselves, and what do you most need from us?

You will notice that these questions are contextual questions about the logo, not necessarily seeking a meeting with the CEO on Day One to discuss their entire business strategy. If you are perceived to be pushing outwards and upwards too much, expect resistance and expect to be blocked.

At the other extreme, many other professionals go straight into logo production (or whatever service they are being asked to perform) *without* asking any contextual questions at all. Instead, all their questions are about scope and *content*, which represents their comfort zone and where they are most at home. Unfortunately for them, the client just perceives a lack of understanding of their needs – and often a lot of indifference, too.

Content questions vs context questions

A content question relates to the content of the work to be done. A context question relates to the context in which that work is being done: for example, why it's important, the other initiatives that are going on around it, the people whose support will be needed, the history of this issue, and anything else that the customer (or you) deem to be relevant.

Though there is usually lots of laughter in our workshops when we come to the exercises around *content* and *context*, it's sometimes tinged with regret as awareness dawns about all the lost opportunity that has resulted from proposals and presentations that have been (alas) too content-heavy, but context-light.

Which of the following questions are context questions?

· What did you think of our presentation/proposal?
· Let's define the scope of the project...
· What's your timescale for delivery?
· What resources are you expecting us to provide?
· What's the next step in the decision making?
· How likely is it that you would recommend us to others?

Short answer: none of these are context questions. They may reflect our real concerns with our services, but none of these questions convey a genuine interest in the customer or their world. Therefore they are not true value-centred questions, as the value of any job always lies in the context in which it is performed, that is, its usefulness, the reason why it's important.

The big ask

> *'What we must decide is perhaps **how** we are valuable, rather than how valuable we are'* - Edgar Friedenberg

Discovering value entails an essential leap into the world of the other, an abandonment of our own self-preoccupation.

This is not easy: neither for individuals nor for companies. It's a Big Ask. Yet it brings a massive boost to motivation. We learn to be interest**ed** rather than trying to be interest**ing**. As we spiral outwards in dialogue – from a genuine preoccupation with adding value, being useful and rendering service – we become trustworthy. Even if the 'farmer' remains suspicious, what matters is the value we bring to his farm, not what he thinks about us.

An idealistic approach? Even those who scoff at the mindset are often won over by the results. In a nutshell, professionals become courageous... often overnight. A value-centred mindset can become so seductive that even scoffers have become converts. Even hardened professionals – who initially learn context questioning just in order to get what they want – can become so intrigued by what they find in the client-world that it rejuvenates their professional lives and raises their energy.

It certainly boosts their courage. There is great freedom in the discovery that other people's opinions about us are simply none of our business. When we are genuinely interested in the client world and the wider marketplace, there are more fruitful things to talk about.

Acknowledgements

We (Kate and John) would both like to thank Philippa Holland for introducing us, also her colleagues Cheryl Coulby, John Appleby and all the consultants with whom we have worked at Bluefin Solutions. Thanks also to all who have played a significant role in the VCO journey to date: Sarah Cronin, Patrice van de Walle, Gerard MacNamara and all at Schuman Associates, Pyramideon in Antwerp and Anete Lejiete for the research, Graham Kennedy, Helen Qubain in Washington, Cristobel Morrison in Singapore, and SWAT UK, particularly Judith Fogarty and Adrian Gibbons.

Thanks to the contributing authors in Part Four and the hundreds of clients whose stories are woven into the fictional characters of this book. While any resemblance to specific persons is certainly accidental, we hope our readers can identify with many of them.

John would like to thank Mary Farmer and Kristin Engvig for planting the seeds in Geneva during WIN 2005, and to all at Success 121 who watered the garden since then: particularly Pam Harris, Dawn Shepherd, John Braught, Andrea Rees, Sara Kinsley and Colette Kwong Hing. Et Sophie et Eléonore pour l'accompagnement pendant la première écriture.

To inspiring friends and associates: Michael Myerscough, Angelika Poltz, Olwyn Merritt, Roland Somville, Plunkett Connolly, Beatrice Detiege, Magnus Almgren, Mei-Yin Teo, Claire Jacq, Cécile Gissot, Gerry Murray, Bernardo Camisão, Borghild Bø, Paula Gardner, Brian Harris, Helen Highley and Francesca Puccio. To my encouraging family: Harry and Jane, to my brothers and my mum in Ireland, and finally to Laura, my muse and editor during those long days of final production.

About the Authors

John Niland is best-known as a conference speaker and coach with VCO Global (www.vco-global.com), focusing on creating opportunity via better dialogue with customers and marketplace.

John graduated in philosophy only to discover that his native Ireland had limited requirements for philosophers in the 1980s and that supply greatly exceeded demand. He hurriedly cross-trained into computer-science and a first career as a systems analyst/project-leader for 15 years, managing pan-European projects for large FMCG, retail and petrochemical organisations until even the money could not induce him to continue. He then set up his own systems company and soon discovered how little he knew about managing people. The real learning began: how to develop business *with* people, rather than *for* them.

Since 2000, John has been coaching others to achieve success, with increasing misgivings about the value of this until he accidently discovered a passion for supporting those 'who wish to contribute rather than just to win, and hence produce some real value'.

In parallel, John is one of the co-founders of the European Forum of Independent Professionals, following twelve years of coaching more than 500 professionals to create more value in their work. Author of *Hidden Value* and *100 Tips to Find Time* (e-books available on www.success121.com), John is passionate about motivating contributors to find meaning in work, creating both economic and social value at the same time, cultivating opportunity and encouraging workplaces.

He now lives in Brussels, from where he does cycling trips to Vietnam, walking trips along the St Jacques de Compostela trail and eating trips wherever there is good food. One of his current projects is connecting professionals to non-profit organisations who need specialist services to increase their capacity to serve, while at the same time enhancing value for contributing professionals.

·····

Kate Daly is an organisation development specialist, coach and psychotherapist. She has 20 years' experience working with a variety of businesses from start-ups to FTSE 100 companies, helping them design and develop their organisations.

As a psychology graduate she started life at Marks & Spencer training in HR management and went on to a commercial role, running stores. She cut her consulting teeth with KPMG running Change and Communications programmes before heading up their Leadership Development practice. She then went and practised what she preached and set up her own business specialising in vision, brand and behaviour; helping CEOs embed strategies for behavioural change that translated into commercial results. During this time she studied for her post-grad in psychology, working with inmates in prison and the public sector.

She is an expert in organisation systems, individual behavioural psychology and change management and spends most of her time working closely with clients' HR and leadership teams to identify the capabilities, organisation structure, roles and processes required to deliver their visions and step-change organisational performance. She also has a one-to-one counselling practice based online and in SW London.

When she's not putting clients' businesses under the microscope, Kate can often be found with one eye through a telescope fulfilling another of her passions, cosmology, and the theory of multiverse (infinite universe, apparently!). Kate lives in SW London with her two young children.

·····

Ronald J. Baker is founder of VeraSage Institute and the best-selling author of *The Firm of the Future: A Guide for Accountants, Lawyers, and Other Professional Services; Pricing on Purpose: Creating and Capturing Value; Measure What Matters to Customers: Using Key Predictive Indicators; Mind Over Matter: Why Intellectual Capital is the Chief Source of Wealth*; and his latest book, *Implementing Value Pricing: A Radical Business Model for Professional Firms*, from which this chapter has been adapted. Email him at Ron@verasage.com and follow his blog at www.verasage.com.

·····

Jan Vermeiren is the founder of Networking Coach, the first LinkedIn Certified Training Institute in the world. An international speaker, Jan is the author of two bestsellers: *Let's Connect!* and *How to REALLY use LinkedIn*. He is also a guest lecturer in several international MBA programmes.

·····

Bert Verdonck is a partner at Networking Coach. As a LinkedIn expert, speaker and author, Bert teaches comfort and success when networking; whether online or offline. Both Jan and Bert work with organisations such as Deloitte, IBM, ING Bank, Mobistar, Nike, SAP, Siemens, as well as small companies and freelancers, and are giving away a million free books, see www.how-to-really-use-linkedin.com for details.

·····

Mary Farmer specialises in workplace innovation: creating high performing teams and inclusive working environments, maximising organisational effectiveness, organisational learning and development and succession and workforce-planning design. Former Director of Diversity and Inclusion for Philips CHRM in Amsterdam, she is presently Executive Director of the Talent and Inclusion Strategy Network for Executive Networks, where she connects the enterprise heads of talent, diversity and inclusion from the largest corporations in the world. Following studies in Journalism and Cultural Anthropology, Mary holds an MBA in International Management from Leiden University and is doctoral candidate in Organisational Behaviour at the University of Amsterdam. She holds dual Canadian and Dutch citizenship and resides in Switzerland, where she heads Online Programs for the Glion Institute of Higher Education and lectures in the university's MBA programs. She speaks fluent English, Dutch, Thai and Bahasa Indonesia, and has working proficiency in Lao, Malay and Flemish. She speaks 'statistically bilingual' Canadian French and a smattering of Mandarin and Spanish.

Index